The Legend of Vortigern

SIMON HEYWOOD

SERIES ORIGINATOR: FIONA COLLINS

To my parents

Illustrations by Samantha Galbraith

First published 2013

The History Press
The Mill, Brimscombe Port
Stroud, Gloucestershire, GL5 2QG
www.thehistorypress.co.uk

British Library Cataloguing in Publication Data.
A catalogue record for this book is available from the British Library.

ISBN 978 0 7524 9004 5

Typesetting and origination by The History Press
Printed in Great Britain
Manufacturing managed by Jellyfish Solutions Ltd

Ancient Legends Retold: An Introduction to the Series

This book represents a new and exciting collaboration between publishers and storytellers. It is part of a series in which each book contains an ancient legend, reworked for the page by a storyteller who has lived with and told the story for a long time.

Storytelling is the art of sharing spoken versions of traditional tales. Today's storytellers are the carriers of a rich oral culture, which is flourishing across Britain in storytelling clubs, theatres, cafés, bars and meeting places, both indoors and out. These storytellers, members of the storytelling revival, draw on books of traditional tales for much of their repertoire.

The partnership between The History Press and professional storytellers is introducing a new and important dimension to the storytelling revival. Some of the best contemporary storytellers are creating definitive versions of the tales they love for this series. In this way, stories first found on the page, but shaped 'on the wind' of a storyteller's breath, are once more appearing in written form, imbued with new life and energy.

My thanks go first to Nicola Guy, a commissioning editor at The History Press, who has championed the series, and secondly to my friends and fellow storytellers, who have dared to be part of something new.

Fiona Collins, Series Originator, 2013

Foreword

Vortigern is an enigma. A figure of rumour from a little-known age; a king of mysteriously questionable standing; a friend of his people's enemies – he is a riddle on more than one count. Even his name has been suspected of being merely a title. It means 'Great Chieftain'.

Like all legends, Vortigern's neglected story hangs in the balance between truth and imagination. His world is Britain in the mid-fifth

century, a few decades after Britain mysteriously dropped off the map of the Roman
Empire. Until the early 400s, Britain was
part of the Roman world: Celtic in heritage
and language, but Christian in religion, and
fairly Latin and literate in education. Then,
shortly after AD 400, something happened.
Exactly what, we don't know. For two cen-
turies afterwards, virtually nobody wrote
anything in or about Britain that we can
still read, and archaeology tells us only so
much. But when the art of writing began to
flourish in Britain again, around AD 600, a
network of Anglo-Saxon kingdoms was settled across the South and East. English was
spoken and written in these kingdoms, and
oral and literate traditions testify to a long,
violent and tumultuous age of migration
and conquest from Northern Europe. The
English had arrived in Britain.

Like Arthur, Vortigern is a British ruler, fea-
turing in legends relating to this mysterious
period. His career is defined by generational

wars, among his own people – the Celtic British – and against the encroaching English. He bulks large in the Matter of Britain, the medieval legend-cycle which numbers Lear, Cymbeline and Arthur amongst its dozens of kings. If Arthur embodies a sense that Britain was hardy enough to flourish even in adversity, Vortigern's voice is an older, more anguished one, closer to the raw shock of Britain's apparent abandonment to her enemies by the ebbing power of Rome. If his age really was a Dark Age, then, unlike Arthur, Vortigern speaks to us bluntly, from the heart of its darkness. Small wonder if he has been ignored; and if not ignored, then usually blamed. But, of the two heroes, Vortigern is the better attested in terms of historical fact, for Gildas mentions him.

Gildas is one of the few writers we know from fifth-century Britain; his work is a Christian denunciation of the British kings and rulers of his own day. Gildas describes an unnamed 'proud tyrant' who took the epochal step of inviting the English to Britain as mercenaries, around the middle of the century. This sounds like it was Vortigern; the description may be a pun on his name.

Vortigern is named in the work of the eighth-century monk-historian Bede, which draws on Gildas' account. Since Bede was English, and Gildas himself appears to have derived some of his knowledge from English sources, there seems to have always been a strong English influence on the extant tales of this British ruler. However, the unknown Welsh author of the ninth-century *History of the Britons* draws on a biography of Vortigern's enemy, St Germanus of Auxerre, to present Vortigern as evil, rather than foolish, unlucky or tragic. Evil is how Vortigern has tended to appear ever afterwards – when he has not been forgotten entirely.

Obscure as he remains, Vortigern has never gone away. People may not know his story nowadays, but they have often heard his name. I already felt vaguely and mysteriously familiar with his name when I first read it in another English source, J.R.R. Tolkien's *The Homecoming of Beorhtnoth Beorhthelm's Son*. There is more to this than the half-after-life Vortigern enjoys as a minor character in modern Arthurian fiction, for his roots run deep. He maintains a presence in Welsh tradition, giving his name to ruins and topo-graphical features (Nant Gwrtheyrn), besides a whole medieval district (Guorthigirniaun) in Powys, of whose royal house he is reckoned to be an ancestor.

This account of Vortigern's legend is based on the best-known medieval version, Geoffrey of Monmouth's twelfth-century *History of the Kings of Britain*. In most respects Geoffrey was a very long way from the real fifth century. But rereading his account, and returning to it repeatedly for guidance, leaves me convinced that he was not a bad historian, as some have thought him, but a storyteller. Or, at the very least, he was a diligent student of storytelling traditions which had harboured Vortigern's tale since its inception, which Professor Ifor Williams places among the *cyfarwyddiaid* – the professional storytellers of medieval Wales. My guess is that some of these masters found Vortigern less flatly wicked than Geoffrey admitted. Accordingly, although I have followed Geoffrey in putting legend before history in my loyalties, I have parted company with him in looking for more than a simple villain behind the mysterious name. But I have not forgotten Vortigern's frailties, or the sorrow of his times. Also, I have sought a glimpse, within the Celtic British heartland, the Albion of legend, of the lost realm which Geoffrey calls Loegria, now lying half-submerged beneath England. Geoffrey, I hope, would approve.

I have done my best to represent legendary Albion in readable terms, but for clarity it may help to note that my Carglu is Geoffrey's Kaerglou – the settlement which the English called Gloucester; Armor is Armorica, or Brittany; Habren is the Severn; the Mor Habren is the Severn Sea – the Bristol

Channel; Rydychen is Oxford; Carguent is Kaerguenit, now Winchester; Car Ebrac is York; Erith is Eryri, that is, Snowdonia; Cernow is Cornwall; Carcaradoc is Salisbury; and Mordun is Carmarthen.

My thanks go to my wife Shonaleigh, for her invaluable comments on early drafts.

Sincere thanks must also go to Nicola Guy at the History Press, and Dr Fiona Collins, the series instigator.

Simon Heywood, 2013

Prologue

Among the western mountains stand the ruins of a tower. Even in your days, you can still see it, if you know where to look. It will strike you as a broken thing, a thing of no account.

Let it. It has weathered storms you know nothing of. And you will think it no more broken than I once thought the ruin of greater things. When I was a man, empires were crumbling which seemed to have lasted since the world began; empires which had been meant to stand forever.

It was wonderful and terrible in those days to listen to the silence that haunted the ruins. Above the wind in the grass around a warlord's abandoned stronghold, or the larks above the broken stones of a hermit's empty chapel, it would seem as if a voice had just fallen silent, after whispering a litany of half-forgotten names: the names of our forefathers of the line of Brutus the old – the high kings and the warriors of Albion.

King as I was myself, I raised the walls of that tower in the western mountains. I raised them with my own hands. And, building them, my hands touched the adorable and pitiless mystery of the world: the mystery of power; the mystery of war; even the mystery of love. And I did not see God face to face; but, before the end came, with my own two waking eyes I saw the great mystery of the created world, like a mingled cloud of mist and fire across the skies. And I held converse with it, and through it I gave Albion her last and greatest blessing.

Everything has been taken from me now.

It is enough for me to foresee you, standing amid the ruins of my tower, catching the echoes of the names of my own friends and servants, and my victims and enemies, and those whose victim I myself became; even perhaps my own name.

My name is Vortigern.

One

Man of the West

When Rome fell, leaving Britain in darkness; when news came no more along the ruined roads and narrow seas, only rumours of war about the palaces of Ravenna, in the long shadow of Attila; when harvests failed, and plague and famine swallowed whole families, houses, and villages – until an unwary traveller might stumble across a silent village of corpses; when silver money grew worthless, and weak as prayer; when outer tribes grew restless again, and harried the coasts of Britain, and beat at the northern wall that Hadrian built; when wealthy townsfolk scavenged for food and fire, and murder was done again for bread or kindling; when the rich buried their gold in their villa gardens, never to unearth it again; in those days, the kings returned to Britain, and ruled its peoples, as they had ruled Albion of old.

The civic councils of Rome could no longer rule the towns, or govern the remote villages or forest peoples. Half-starved councillors continued to issue Latin proclamations which were barely read. Outside the council chambers, men of another kind were beginning to lord it over the common peoples. In the space of a few short years, there was scarcely a household or village in Britain that did not bow in fear to them. Only the bishops and church-priests condemned their sins, because they envied their burgeoning power.

At first, the warlords were no more than petty kings. They could not withstand the tribes that battered the northern wall and the eastern coasts, or the slave raiders of the north-west; they were too busy quarrelling with each other, for wealth and power, land and grain, ships and trade routes, ore from the mines, and slaves from the mountains. Some were no more than nameless brigands. But many bore the names of kings who had reigned in Britain before Rome was made. The old chieftains had faded into the grass when Rome came. But when Rome fell, their grandsons came out of hiding, and crowned themselves kings.

So it was often said, at least. It is easy to lie about one's ancestry when one has a sword to make good the lie. But I truly believe that the blood of Brutus the old, the founder of Britain, did run in the veins of some of the warlords, though it did not make them better men.

And since my own father had no such blood in his veins that anyone knew of, the old chieftains called him a common brigand and tyrant when he finally put down the city council in

Carleon in the west, and took the wild hinter-
lands under his protection, and so became ruler
of a new little kingdom, which inherited the
name of Gwent.

Carleon was worth holding on to: it was
like a little Rome in the wilderness, a refuge
of quiet and order and learning. Our most
powerful neighbours, the chieftains of Carglu,
were children of Brutus the old by name and
line. But they lived in an open sty on a hilltop,
penned in under the sky like beasts, behind
earthen ring-ditches and ramparts which
they believed were the tracks of old dragons
from before the flood. And they lived by pil-
laging their own peoples in village and forest,
and they still feared and hated stone houses
as their forefathers had. And these were the
people who called us tyrants.

But my story is part of the story of the chieftains, new and old, so I will begin it with the
best of them: Constantine, of the house of
Conan, who was king far off to the east, in
London, when I was a boy.

Constantine was a very rich lord in Armor, across the narrow seas. The lords of Armor held all the coasts of Gaul; they were the richest lords in all the West. Britain was no great matter to them. Constantine could have taken Rome itself by conquest. But the church-priests of London offered him the throne in fear of the British warlords, and he took it.

Stranger though he was by birth, Constantine ruled as a true king. He married a British queen. She bore him an heir, a son who spoke British, and they called this boy Constans after his father. But despite his name, he was such a born idiot that they had to make a monk of him, and all London soon forgot him.

For a while, the king was too busy to father more sons. He was forcing peace on the quarrelling warlords. He even herded them into a kind of council: his Long Table, he called it. This pleased the priests who had invited him, and it was a wonder to the poor people. Constantine protected the churchless priesthoods, too: the hermits and holy people, the hedge-priests and mountain-priests and street-preachers, who had roamed the villages and towns for generations without ever setting foot within a stone church, each doing his own service to his own Lord Christ.

When all these things were done, Constantine brought treasure and men from Armor, and marched north to face the tribes. Constantine called these new legions his Household Gauls. The warlords, newly penned in around Constantine's Long Table, hated and feared them. But within the space of a few summers, the Household Gauls had humbled and overthrown the outer tribes and the slave-raiders. Constantine made a peace so generous that even his old enemies acknowledged his friendship. For a few brief summers, it must have seemed that the heyday of Rome had come again.

On his return from the North, Constantine made up for lost time in other matters, and the queen soon bore him twins: healthy, strong-willed sons, whom he christened

Aurel and Uther. They were the only lawful brothers Constans the monk was ever to have. My father met them as children, and he would often say to me that either or both of them might easily take the throne of London one day, when they came to manhood. Constantine established the infant twins with their mother, in a household of their own, some way north of London. He had them brought up by tame priests and powerful friends. Among these friends were the chieftains of Carglu; but there was little that we in Gwent could do about that.

But, like many kings, Constantine grew reckless. He even brought a squadron of Picts to London, to serve in his personal bodyguard alongside the Household Gauls. This was needless. The Household Gauls were protection enough for him; and the Household Gauls hated the Picts. Worse, he brought the Picts south only to taunt the Long Table, to show the chieftains that they were little more than courtiers now.

I was a young man then. I knew little of anything but Gwent's little wars among the peoples of the western mountains and the valley of the great river Habren. My father had married me early, and I was a father already myself; indeed, I was a widower, for my poor wife died young. But I had been so busy in my father's service that I was almost a stranger to sons I loved more than I knew. And so, when my father died, he left no one to take power in Gwent other than myself, and so I took it. I became lord in Carleon. My life began late, and I had half my years behind me before I learned things that others know in youth. There was a price to pay for that, and I paid it.

The chieftains of Carglu were eyeing the little jewel of Carleon even while my father was still alive. No sooner was my father buried than they began to call me tyrant in my turn. That was ominous, so I thought best to ride to London as soon as I could, and ask King Constantine for protection, face to face. I left

Gwent, and crossed the angry sea of the Mor Habren. Giving Carglu as wide a berth as I could, I then took the Roman road which ran among the Thames valley kindreds: small peoples who might have been surprised to learn that Carglu claimed their overlordship. I was already a great enough man to have a good armed guard with me, but none of us had ever yet been to London.

We were still a day's ride from Lud's Gate, by the guides' reckoning, when we met with three laden wagons coming the other way along the road. They were ox carts of middling size, driven by shabbily dressed men: poor eastern merchants, by the look of them. In my grandfathers' days it would not have been strange to see traffic like that on the roads. We hailed the men, and I had the chief of them brought to me, and asked him his errand and his news.

'The king of London is dead,' the merchant told me, in a frightened whisper, as if he was afraid for the trees by the roadside to overhear him.

'King Constantine is dead. The Picts have murdered him.'

He asked our protection, there and then. The man was no fool; it took shrewdness to live as a merchant when life and luxury and money itself were already growing cheap. But he was frightened out of his wits. He seemed to think the port of London was already overrun with bloodthirsty warlords and Pictish pagans. I half-believed him, but we left him to take his chances, and quickened our pace, and rode through the night toward Lud's Gate to see if he was telling the truth.

And he was, in part at least. London was not, in fact, overrun with Picts, or warlords, but the city was in uproar. We had no time to admire the gates and walls and decaying palaces; the townsfolk took us for greater men than we were, and mobbed us from Lud's Gate to the Basilica of Concord, calling on our help and protection. We almost trampled them under our horses' hooves. Everyone we met with told the same tale: King Constantine had been murdered by a Pict of his own household guard. The heathen tribes had feigned friendship, and taken their revenge at last on the reckless king.

We came to the Basilica of Concord, anyway, and found that the king was dead indeed. He was lying in state in his private chambers – and a poor state it was, for his mangled body had been plundered already, and there was only one old woman in attendance on him, an old slave who had been a nun. She was weeping over the king's bier with unfeigned grief. The priests of the Old Temple Church were making arrangements for the funeral, she told me. The murderer was indeed one of the new Picts; he had knifed his new master by stealth in the walled Basilica garden. There had been skirmishing then in the Basilica between the Picts and the Household Gauls, and amid the confusion the guilty man had made his escape. That was two days before, and the assassin was still at large.

I quickly paid my respects to the dead king, gave the woman a brooch, and left.

Amid the turmoil, the business of government seemed to have ceased altogether. Most of Constantine's slaves and ministers seemed to be hiding. The few I could find were all so terrified that they made me feel uneasy myself. I found a slave – a sweeper of some sort, he seemed to be – and frightened him into talking. All he would do was whimper,

'Are you Lord Eldol?'

I had to laugh grimly at this. The terrible Eldol, of course, was neither Pict nor Gaul, but a very British warlord: the chieftain of Carglu himself. The king's servants were frightened of the king's own courtiers. As I supposed they might well be. Eldol and a dozen other warlords and chieftains were rumoured to be almost at the gates of the city, and nobody knew what the great men of Britain would do now the old king was dead.

Anyone with any sense would have gone straight to the Household Gauls. So I did.

The Household Gauls were keeping to their barracks. This struck me as very strange.

Happily, the mere mention of Carleon gained me an audience with General Gralann, for Gauls still respected Carleon a little in those days, ironically enough.

General Gralann was very angry and impatient; also, seemingly, he was drunk. He had done nothing for two days, he spat, because he hated Britain, as he had hated Constantine's meanness, and he was in two minds whether or not to stay here at all.

'My men are no traitors, and no fools,' he declared, in the halting British of the many foreigners in London. He slouched forward on his elbows until the table creaked, and saw he had jostled his cup, and scrutinised the spilled wine with great interest a moment, and went on: 'No traitors. They followed Constantine from a good country. To this pigsty of an island. And then he gave them nothing. Nothing! We have lived here many days. The king's enemies, they were our enemies. And his meat was our meat, and his drink was our drink, and his house was our house.

And he gave us no land. No name of our own, no house of our own. We have lived like common legionaries in the barracks. So it is enough.' He slouched forward again, and stared at me intently, wagging a finger. 'Today and tomorrow, the men will obey me well. But the day after tomorrow? They will kill me with their own hands if I do not do something. It is nature. They cannot eat the name of a dead king. They cannot marry the name of a dead king, or give the name of a dead king for their children to eat.'

'But you could be king in London yourself tomorrow. If you wanted,' I pointed out.

His stare grew more intense.

'A warrior of Armor,' he spat, 'and a chieftain of the house of Conan, does not want to be king in this pigsty of an island! I want to go home before I die. I want to live as rich as a lord, all of my days, and I want to go home to Armor, to die a rich man under the sun. If I am king in Britain, I can never leave Britain again. I want the king of London to give me some land here, and a wife. I do not want to live here. A king in London of Constantine's blood. That is what I want. Son, cousin, brother. Anything. Any such blood is good enough for London. Constantine was a fool, to be killed in such a way. But I got his stupid Picts,' he belched. 'They are in the cellar here, soiling themselves like frightened children. Tomorrow I will kill them all.'

'So,' I suggested, with some tact, 'if that is what you want, a king of the blood of Constantine, then why not crown his sons in London? The twins, Uther and Aurel. And serve them.'

Gralann did even not bother to laugh.

'I am not going to play games with these people, or wait on them hand and foot, for them to finish their games,' he said, as if he was talking to himself. Then he glanced up at me, seeming to remember that I was there. 'The queen and the little princes were in a church, with monks. North of here, in some place. Rydychen. Now they are gone. Eldol has taken them, I think. If he has the princes of the blood, he can get London. That is what he thinks.' Something seemed to strike him then, and he went on, with a shrug: 'Or perhaps he has killed them already. When the king died, I sent men on horses to find them, the little princes, because I know Eldol: he is an old robber. But they were gone. He had got them. I was too slow. I had to stay in London to fight all the stupid Picts.'

For a moment I searched for a reply.

'Do you think Eldol knew the Picts would kill the king?' I asked at last.

Gralann did not trouble to answer this either. He sat almost bolt upright and stared at me, as if he had suddenly been struck with an idea. His eyes were wide and glittering. 'I know!' he said. 'The mad monk. The mad monk can be king. He is of the blood. He is good enough for London. That will fox Eldol. Everyone has forgotten the mad monk. But I remember.'

My heart leaped.

'Let me go for him,' I blurted out. 'The mad monk. Constans. Let me fetch him. He can be king. And then you can stay in London and serve him … since Gwent –'

'How many men do you have, man of Carleon?' he broke in, his face brightening. 'Perhaps I will send men with you. If you go to Carguent and fetch the monk. Then take the monk to the priests of London, and let them put God's blessing on him, as a king must have, before any of the British robbers come to London.' He gripped my arm. 'Then Eldol can do as he pleases with his little princes!'

This seemed to decide him. He leaned back, and stretched.

'And if the priests will not crown the monk,' he yawned, 'then I will go home to Armor. And then I will go wherever they send me. Maybe Ravenna. Maybe Rome. Or Constantinople. Then all the Picts and savages in the world can have this pigsty of an island. And I will laugh. Three days now we have sat here in London like fools, doing nothing, and we are the best men of arms in all the empire.'

I took a squadron of the Household Gauls, and a handful of my own men, and rode to Carguent in search of Constans the monk, to crown him king of London.

I am older and wiser now, and I recognise my mood in those days for what it was. It was the ecstasy which persuades the gambler, in the moment before his fingers release the dice, that good luck attends him. Many die without ever knowing that feeling. But, once known, it is never forgotten. And those who know it are those who stake everything, and throw the dice with a flourish. Such people are the truly great ones, the ones who make the world what it is. They are the bringers of glory; they are the people about whom stories are told. For sometimes the dice obey blindly as they roll, as the world obeyed the voice of God in the beginning.

And in that hour of darkness and confusion, I began to think of myself as one of them.

For I was beginning to understand the mystery of things then, and I was in love with my purpose.

And that, I suppose, was how I first set foot to the road that led me to the feet of dragons.

The cloister at Carguent was an old Roman country house, which had stood empty before the church-priests took it. Now it was a very strange and shabby place, where none but monks would ever think of dwelling. Thankfully we did not need to stop long. It was not hard to browbeat the abbot into letting me see the king's brother. I was invited to wait in a bare, shadowless chamber that might once have been a dining room.

Constans met me there. In the flesh, he was a pale, young man with dark rings around his eyes. He was not mad, I thought, but he certainly was a spoiled monk: a childish man, who hated the cloister and knew nothing else. When I told him that he was king in London, he did not idle. We brought him in secret to the Basilica, and I went at once to see the Archbishop of London, to crown him, as Gralann the general wished.

The archbishop in those days was a rich old church-priest who had taken the church-name of Amphibalus; I never learned his birth name. I told Amphibalus that the safety of the realm depended on the Household Gauls. The Gauls would not remain in London without a crowned king of the blood of Constantine, I said. The little twin princes were missing, I said; perhaps they were dead already. I proposed that he should crown the monk, Constans. I heard a weak echo of Gralann's voice in my own words as I spoke.

The archbishop stood by the window, making a show of listening. Then he sighed, closed the shutters on the noisy London streets below, and turned to face me.

'Constans,' he explained, 'has taken very serious and binding vows. He is a monk now.'

'Don't mock me with religion, Holy Father, I said. 'If Constans remains a monk –'

The archbishop turned and gave me a piercing stare. 'Who are you, man of the west?' he asked. 'Are you a king or a lord of the blood of Brutus? Or are you a common thief's brat and brigand, wearing a stolen crown? A friend of hedge-priests and blasphemers? What are you?'

'I do not think there is a word for what I am,' I said, with the best grace I could manage.

'The chieftains of Carglu have a word for what you are,' he said at once.

So I found that the archbishop would not crown the monk. But I did not think General Gralann of the Household Gauls, warrior and chieftain of Armor, would care so much what a mere bishop thought. And I could not afford to idle, for rumour was that the warlords were almost at the gates.

So, God help me, I made Constans a king of London without troubling the church further for its help. I crowned Constans king of London with my own hands the very next day, under an overcast sky, in the chief marketplace of the city. A scattered crowd watched from a distance, and gave the new king a ragged cheer. Then, jubilantly, I sent word to General Gralann at his barracks at the Basilica.

I achieved one thing: the warlords and chieftains, who were spreading such fear around the Basilica, melted away without showing their faces, for they sensed that Constans the monk might be king enough now for London.

But of course Gralann the general was not British. Gralann was a man of Armor, after all: that vast, slow, cunning, wicked power. And I did not appreciate the standing of bishops and church-priests in Gaul, who are great lords themselves, and the equals of the Gaulish kings. It would have been a joke to any Gaulish general to suppose that a man such as I could crown a king. The Household Gauls sailed for Armor with the tide. They left us to the marauding tribes and squabbling warlords. The Pictish soldiers were still starving in the cellar of the barracks; General Gralann had not even bothered to kill them.

So began the reign of Constans, king of London. From the outset, the strange little king was beset by enemies, bereft of warriors, and condemned by the church.

And from the outset I was always by his side. And that was how I began: burning with a purpose I only half-understood, saddled with the first of my great failures, amid storm clouds which were already gathering over my head.

Two

A Hide of Land

But that, I think, was how I stopped a war for the throne of London.

It was a close-run thing. I was marooned alongside Constans in the friendless east, far from home. Just the kind of man the greater eastern chieftains despised: a westerner, an upstart, and a commoner, neither truly British, as they saw it, nor truly Roman.

My sons remained in Carleon. I could happily have run back to Gwent myself, but

I would surely have been hunted down. I hardly dared leave the Basilica, let alone leave London. I left the state rooms to King Constans and his new friends, and camped out amid the dust and the lumber and the rats of the galleries under the dome. I was desperate for friends. If I could have found giants or dragons still at large in Albion, I would have made common cause with them, against Eldol, if I could.

In these troubled times I found that there was an old library in an attic under the rafters of the Basilica. Libraries have always been wonderful places to me, because I have never understood how books work. No sooner had I found it than I went looking in it for tales of priest-kings of old, for I thought in my ignorance that it could not be hard to make books yield up their stories, even for an unlettered man. I had no idea what I was dealing with. All I could do was stare dumbly at the woven marks on the pages.

But as I stared, I discerned a cloaked man standing some way off between the shelves, in the half-shadow of my lantern.

The man was keeping his distance; whether warily or respectfully, I could not tell. I could still see that he wore the trimmed black robe of the sarabaites, the black hermits – the greatest of the churchless priesthoods of Albion in learning and authority. Now, of course, in those days, I was on my guard against assassins every day. But this sarabaite did not seem to be much of an assassin. So I called out testily: 'Who are you there?'

'Maugan, sire,' came a thin, reedy voice. 'They call me the Scribe.'

'They call you the Scribe?' The phrase sounded strange to my ears.

The man stirred nervously in the shadows, shuffling his weight from foot to foot, and I could not help thinking he seemed about to make a faintly embarrassing confession. I prepared to defend myself nonetheless, in case he meant violence. But still he did not strike.

'Sire,' he called out, very cautiously, 'it has come to my attention that there is an inn on Belin's Way, outside Car Ebrac on the south, where, if you look quickly, you will find the man who murdered the late king.' I must have looked astonished, but the man did not seem to notice; at least, he did not pause. 'The assassin is hoping to cross the borderlands in the next day or two. He is a Pict, of course. If you send riders now, he will be yours. The best horseman, riding post-haste from London with fresh horses, could be in Car Ebrac by midday tomorrow. And the assassin is delayed there, waiting for an accomplice. A guide, who knows the northern kindreds. The name and sign of the inn is the Wheel. It is well enough known among travellers in the North.'

He stopped, and coughed, and swallowed, and waited. After a moment, I asked him bluntly: 'And how do you claim to know all this, Scribe?'

He made what seemed to be a noncommittal gesture.

'Did you read it in one of these books?'

He took a few steps towards me. I bridled.

'Sire,' he replied, in a more confiding tone, 'I am coming towards the end of a lifetime's service in this library, and, these days, I find little to admire beyond its narrow walls. But to those whom I do admire, I can offer service of value. Immense value. I have waited here since the old king died, and I have watched the new king, Constans, and the manner of his accession. I can help you, sire. Spare a handful of riders for four days. It is not hard. Trust me this once.'

I was unaccustomed then to the company of really cultivated men, but I sensed the candour in his strange manner.

And that was my first meeting with Maugan the Scribe. I sent the riders as he advised, and before the week was out, I had the murderer chained in the cellars. I questioned him without mercy. Maugan helped me with that, too – he brought me a Pictish interpreter.

'King Constantine forbade interpreters,' he said, acidly. 'He liked being the only man in the palace who could understand the Picts.'

The interpreter was a dark, wiry, nervous youth, whom Maugan called Calgac. Calgac, I learned, had served the Pictish chiefs loyally through a number of bitter feuds and wars in the North, before being captured and sold to a chieftain south of the wall, from whom Maugan had bought him, more or less. Calgac revealed himself to be the kind of man who would always behave with passionate and unthinking devotion to whichever object of loyalty happened to be nearest at the time – which, of course, as long as I knew him, was me. I wondered how he felt about playing the interpreter as I interrogated his countryman under torture. He was melancholy, but seemed determined to put a brave face on it.

There was nothing to be got from the assassin; the man was acting out of passion for the honour of his people, and that was all there was to it. I had to hang him. And I found that this simple act of bloodletting freed my hand.

Constantine's Pictish bodyguards were still languishing in the cellars below the barracks. Within days of the executions, I turned their luck for them. Beneath their misery, the Picts were real hills-men. I had grown up fighting

with hills-men, and against them: such were
the men of Erith, near Gwent, who had always
come and gone between Carleon and the valleys, to brawl and deal in cattle and attend to
the affairs of their own kindreds. Now, I had
Calgac tell the Picts that I was the London king's
chief servant, and that I now had Constantine's
murderer in chains. I was willing to hold them
blameless of the old king's death – provided,
that is, that they put aside the old feud with the
house of Constantine, and remained in London
as the new king's household regiment. I gave
them my word on it; mine, not the king's. But
if they were to hold to the feud, I went on, they
could expect death for themselves at once, and
war for their kindreds. This threat was a lie,
one of the few straight lies I ever told. In those
days we could not have made war without the
Picts – still less against them.

The Pictish commanders listened sullenly,
and debated among themselves at length,
rattling their chains with their extravagant
gestures. Calgac wept with joy as he told me

of their agreement to my plan. Overnight, we got King Constans a small, ragged, ready-made army. By themselves, they were just able to keep order in the London streets, and no more. But they had clansmen in the North in their thousands.

'Enough to divide and rule all the warlords in Britain,' Maugan said.

'No,' I told him, grimly. 'Enough to buy us a little time to find better friends.'

He knew this already, really; in his good moods, he was fond of deliberate overstatement.

Word went quickly north beyond the wall that Constantine's heir in London had a powerful servant who was a friend. I gave the Pictish chiefs in the North a free hand, to encourage them to hold off their feud with the Constantines. I had to swallow my anger when the chiefs ransacked the North. I knew it was necessary to let them.

'Although you will pay for it,' Maugan warned me. He gave a very wan smile. 'The best soldiers do tend to make the worst neighbours.'

'And the worst traitors,' I said. I sighed. 'Let us just hope we are prepared by the time they turn.'

At least the holy people of Britain prospered by us, better than the Picts. Since King Constans and I had publicly flouted the bishops, small shrines and chapels sprang up even in London. My favourite among these vagabond-saints was a shrivelled old man, hardly bigger than a child, clearly one of the northern forest peoples, who would ply his trade day and night in London market, beating a drum and singing, and selling cures and blessings. He seemed to have, and want, no other home. He adored a being which he called the Christ-Sun-Day, whose image adorned a crude placard which he would prop up against the wall. My old friend Bles Gwin, the hedge-priest's son, was soon learning tales of saints and miracles in London to his heart's content.

Maugan oversaw all of this: Maugan the Scribe; Maugan the dweller in shadows, the educated man, the pitiless inquisitor, the clever spy. He was always close-mouthed about himself, but he seemed to have been at the library since youth. Slowly, over the years, he told me, he had discovered a supreme talent for stealth. He had thought Constantine a fool and a braggart, and had long since foreseen his death. When the young Pict had struck him down, Maugan had simply locked himself in the Molmutine Library, and waited.

Maugan never willingly left his beloved library, but he had eyes and ears in every court. He made his mistakes, but mostly, if all the birds of Britain had sung him the news each morning, he could not have learned it more swiftly, or more surely.

I had a permanent apartment set up in the high gallery, and was soon speaking with Maugan daily. Thanks to the Scribes – as we called his secret army of informers – we learned that the twins had really been in the cloister all the time, under chieftain Eldol's fosterage. Eldol had not killed them. The queen was in a nunnery. In all but name, the twins and their mother were pris-

oners of Gwent's enemies, in their stronghold on
the grass-green dragon-hill of Carglu.

But that knowledge enabled me to summon
the grim old chieftain Eldol from his dragon-hill
to London, and upbraid him in the king's name.
Eldol listened impassively, with his arms folded:
a granite-faced mountain of a man, who looked
faintly ridiculous in the long moustache which
he cherished in order to proclaim his British
ancestry. For all my huffing and puffing, I had
to appoint Eldol guardian to the twin princes.
Beyond making it very slightly more difficult for
him to kill them, this made no real difference.
We had Maugan's Scribes watch the twins.

King Constans wanted the twins killed. He
also wanted the Picts massacred, and said so
openly, once or twice. I berated him, but as
far as he was concerned, he was the king, and
could say what he liked. Constans must have
made a pretty poor monk.

He paid the price in the end; and so did I.
Calgac the interpreter walked in on me one

evening when I was working – finally thinking of crossing the narrow seas as I had promised myself, and looking to the future. Calgac had something bulky with him, wrapped in a cloak. I could almost smell the fear and anger and excitement. I was ready to fight him at once.

'Are you going to cross the sea?' he asked nervously.

I did not answer. He unwrapped his cloak, and set the severed head of King Constans on the gilded table. I stared. For an instant, I could not breathe.

'Do not leave,' he said. 'Stay with us. You are the strongest now! Be king!'

Afterwards, I could always recall every detail of the dead king's face: the eyelids, untidily half-closed; the slobbering lips; the absurdly peaceful loneliness of the shoulderless head, resting on a huge throat wound like a one-lipped mouth.

I knew at once that my friendship with the Picts was over, and I was prey to the warlords. My life at that moment might well depend on not wasting precious time on rage. I forced myself to breathe, and then, very quietly, I asked him: 'You did this?'

He nodded.

'Who else have you told?'

'Nobody.'

'And nobody else knows? No-one has seen?'

'No.'

I dragged Calgac to the dungeons with my own hands. Once I had him prisoner, I had time for anger. I took my time. By the time I left him, his own mother would scarcely have recognised him.

I went back with Maugan the next day, and we went to work again, with questions. The truth was bleak, but simple. Calgac had killed Constans out of love for me; he thought I would be pleased, and would stop seeking other warriors and servants to replace his poor, beloved Picts.

I hanged Calgac from the walls of London, and buried Constans in the Temple Church alongside his father. I permitted Archbishop Amphibalus to take the funeral. My two elder sons were in

London by then, because up until the king's death I had thought the town a little safer. Now they stood beside me in the Old Temple Church before the ragged choir: Vortimer, a handsome, nervous boy of thirteen, with his chubby, red-haired brother Catigern clinging to his arm.

And then, of course, the people turned on the Picts. As the grim days passed, news came of reprisals and murders all across Britain. I nearly lost control of the London streets. I was desperate. I even called a Long Table in London to debate the succession. But by the time it gathered, I saw too late that there was no use in caution; for already there was another disaster to face.

Archbishop Amphibalus did not attend the Long Table. He had caught Maugan's Scribes napping, and fled London on the day after the funeral, before dawn, on horseback, with a handful of attendants. I had the coasts watched.

How bitterly now I wish I could have watched them closer. Maugan by now was counting our enemies on his fingers.

'The lords of Armor and the Household Gauls. Bishop Amphibalus and the church-priests ...' He paused, and swallowed very nervously, and announced: 'And I am afraid we can probably add the house of Constantine to the list. The twins are missing from Rydychen: the little princes, Aurel and Uther. I –'

My heart nearly stopped.

'What?' I shouted.

'I suspect they are in Armor now. I think. I am awaiting final proof, but ... Amphibalus was cleverer than I thought. Cleverer than Eldol thought, too, it seems.'

It turned out to be true: Amphibalus had taken the twin princes. Now they were guests – that is, prisoners – of their kinsman, the new lord of Armor. Losing an archbishop was nothing; losing twin princes was terrible. I made Maugan find out which of his Scribes had failed to see this coming, and told him to poison them. He knew I meant it, and he did it.

All I could do besides was summon Eldol privately and demand to know what had become of his duty to foster and protect the princes. The old chieftain silently put on a face like thunder, let me rant, and then turned on his heel and walked out of the chamber of audience without a word. I seemed the least of his worries. I was truly afraid, as I richly deserved to be.

'What we failed to see was that Eldol and Amphibalus have fallen out,' Maugan said. 'Amphibalus has picked his pockets and taken his princes. Eldol has just let a great chance slip through his fingers.'

'As have we,' I told him. 'But it doesn't matter now. What matters is I need a king in London, with an army.' I sighed. 'It will take a miracle.'

But once again, I felt the touch of the gambler's ecstasy, which gives the dice the extra dash of grace as the fingers release them. And now I felt it a second time, I understood it better. For I had nursed my little King Constans through the dangers of war and turmoil, and I new now pretty well that one day I, like him, would die for the sake of the purpose I had taken in hand. But I had tasted a little luck now, and I surprised myself with the ferocity of the passion I felt for my purpose. For I accepted now that the ecstasy that drove me was a call to embrace death. I was already the father of sons, but still I had not yet known that fear of death which lies at the heart of love.

I needed a miracle, and, having no other choice, I courted that miracle by an act of will. I took the throne, and became a usurper outright, thinking that if I was to die, I might as well die a king.

Snow fell on London the day I crowned myself. The hooves of the horses were muffled in the streets, and the people lined the streets and watched sullenly as I made my way under the canopy to the Heartstone, walled in by veils of falling snow.

And once I was king, I had my miracle. Warriors flocked to my banner: cruel and outlandish men enough, to offer to old Albion as her saviours.

The first that London heard was news from a rider from the coastguards. Some days before, three longships had made landfall on the southern shore, and the seafarers had been given safe conduct through the villages to London gates. I had already heard a whisper from the Scribes, and I was already waiting.

After some days more, the strangers arrived in London, marching with an escort of coastguards from Cent through the cluttered London streets, with pale, blue eyes in weathered faces, and rolling gait, and bright shirts of mail, and long fair hair. The sea air still clung to them, and the air of a land I could not place or name. They gazed up at me impassively with folded arms from the floor of the Basilica of Concord, while my court, such as it was, looked on. The headmen seemed to be twins, or brothers; their hair was white as fleece, although they were youngish men. They spoke through an interpreter, a nervous, intelligent-looking British prisoner. I never knew this man's name, for the strangers only called him Welc.

'We are Juten,' said Welc, translating the elder chieftain's words. 'Hengest is my name. We have left our homeland according to custom. There are too many young men among us, and too much war. At such times we draw lots and the best men take to the seas. We have come here. We seek service with kings.'

I offered them bed and board at the Basilica, and promised them an answer on the third morning. They spent the days eating and drinking moderately at my table, basking in the apprehensive stares of the court and the city.

'A chieftain was killed in the North lately, I believe,' Maugan told me dryly, amid the shadows of the Molmutine. 'Some months ago. By men who were staying with him as his own guests. It happens from time to time in the longhouses of the far North, sire, though it's always seen as a great crime. It stands to reason that the killers, whoever they were, would have every reason to be looking for a new life far from home. They would be shunned by all who had known them.'

'How do you know this?' I demanded.

'I know the North a little,' Maugan said, with his diffident shuffle of the feet. 'From traders and whale-fishers, ultimately. The Greek authors we have in the library. The main thing is they seem to know nothing of Christ. They worship devils, as I suppose you might say. But if pagans are willing to learn a little of the black arts of tact and discretion from their devils, they can make acceptable mercenaries for a Christian king. If they plan on settling permanently,' he gave a shrug, 'it would be a different matter. Perhaps they might be interested in conversion,' he added wistfully.

'I would love them to plan on settling permanently,' I said, 'if they are men of their word, and as fierce as they look. They could even take the place of the Household Gauls. God knows we have done what we can with the Picts, but really it is a wonder we are still here at all. As you well know. I am sure Eldol would have tried to finish us off by now, if he still had the twins. And God knows he would have been in with a chance.'

On the third day, I met with Hengest and Horsa in a private chamber of audience, just abutting on the main hall. In private, they spoke some British. I was not altogether surprised. We soon understood each other perfectly, and the matter was easily settled.

'I will not lie to you,' I told Hengest. 'I cannot make you many promises. But I can make some, and you will find that I am a man of my word. I give you a roof over your heads. Meat and drink. I pay you in gold. You do no public dishonour to the churches of Christ, or the priesthoods of Christ. After one war, we speak again. One war. One battle. You and me together, against my enemies.'

'Who are your enemies?' Hengest said.

'The Picts,' I told him. 'The Picts now. Later, others,' I added, thinking of Eldol. 'A king has many enemies.'

Hengest put his hand to his neck and pulled out a small amulet of dull iron. It looked like a cross. He held it up. Horsa did likewise.

'Then the Picks are our enemies,' Hengest said carefully. 'Now. Later, perhaps, others. I do not lie.'

Then, with Hengest and Horsa's help, I marched North at last, and turned on the Picts for the sake of the British.

The memory of that Pictish war was a joy to me for a long time after. After all my waiting and scheming and shame, I was back on horseback, with the weight of a spear in my hand, riding into the approaching storm. I left the British warlords like housewives at home.

We fought in small, fast-moving squadrons, moving northward from Car Ebrac along the vale towards the high country before the wall, relying heavily on the land and the peoples of the villages. We were received coolly at first. To the common kindreds of the North, Hengest and Horsa seemed scarcely less outlandish than the Pictish enemy. And I was an old friend of the Picts: we had to betray some who trusted us, just as we had to use force against the weak. But there is a kind of pleasure even in the squalid traffic of war, if it is skilfully handled. And we proved our worth to the villagers once the fighting began. By the end of the summer, we wanted for neither bed nor bread, nor news nor warnings, nor places to rest and hide, nor men to fill the places of the dead and wounded in our ranks, nor a welcome anywhere among the Northern peoples. And I had learned that the strongest allies in any war – or in any peace – are the many who never hold a weapon in their hands. I might add that children were kindly begotten in their dozens on British mothers during that war, and many had the fair hair and blue eyes of Hengest's men.

We did more than challenge the Picts: we drove them back to the wall. They were accustomed to hilly terrain, but they were not used to holding any territory against massed ranks. So it was easy to take land from them, even their own mountains; but harder to hold it against them, once taken.

I feared at first that Hengest and his men would be out of place, for they rode no horses, and mountains were things they knew nothing of, and they had little skill in skirmishing.

But we grew adept at using British cavalry to herd the enemy towards Hengest's solid shield-wall, where his men would then hack them to pieces. In the rush of the skirmish, I was often left behind, but even around the shoulders of northern hills I learned to rejoice at the sound of Hengest's war cry when this slaughter commenced: *Nemethur saxa! Seize axes!* Our men began to call Hengest's men Nimadders, Nimaddersaxans, and finally, simply, Saxans. And even when they became a people – though they called themselves otherwise – they were white Saxans to the British, ever afterwards.

Around the white Saxans' campfires, I learned a little of their ways. They were a taciturn lot, but they had pride. Whatever they did, they did with dignity, even down to their drinking: our ears grew accustomed to their wass-hails and drinc-hails and other healths.

Amid the fortunes of war, Hengest never allowed anything to disquiet him. He never smiled, but shrugged often. He could be cruel by day and sleep soundly at night, a skill which

Maugan had, and I lacked. He never turned a guest away and he never failed to revenge an injury. But heathen as he was, he retained a kind of alert sympathy for all men equally, as the toys of fate; even for his enemies as he butchered them. And he had not lied: the Picts were now his enemies, and he cleared them from the North as he might have cleaned the lice from his shirt. His brother seemed more open-hearted, a hardy fighter who depended on his brother in everything.

I brought my sons with me eagerly, entertaining high hopes of them, now they were old enough to join with me in my work. But Vortimer wearied the whole army with his brattishness. It was an ugly and dispiriting spectacle he made, and I sent him back to Car Ebrac on a pretext long before the war was over. He threw a tantrum even at this, and tried to refuse to go.

But Catigern, who seemed a simpleton, a poor chubby copy of his handsome brother, had wits enough to command a troop of horse before he had a beard on his cheek. He stayed, although he missed his brother.

We made war for all of the brief northern summer, and did well. Then we came south again as the nights began to draw in, moving down the eastern coasts and hanging pirates whenever we could find them. They were easy times, the nearest I ever came to happiness in all of my kingship. I had almost forgotten about the dragon-hill fortress of Carglu, except to think of it from time to time as a den of vanquished bandits.

The Saxan brothers and I spoke again privately on this journey.

'I do not lie, king,' Hengest repeated. 'I see now you have many enemies. More than a king should have. The Picks on the wall: you need to watch them. And the pirates from the sea: you need to fight them. And British enemies, your own people,' he added, to my surprise. 'And the people over the seas.' His eye glittered as he spoke. 'You need friends. And I have friends.

There are many more of us. More at home, in the North.'

'How many more?' I asked casually. I tried to be cautious, but it was the offer I had dreamed of.

'Many hundreds more,' he said. Then he hesitated. 'But I must give them something. A sign.'

'A sign?'

As we approached London, he became more forthcoming.

'We have a custom,' he said. 'A hide of land. It is like this: a man wants to live in your country. You want him, but not too rich, too strong. You give him a raw ox hide. And you say: take one hide of land! It is a contest, a test for him. He stretches the hide with his hands, he is strong enough! He puts the hide on the ground and takes the land that goes under it. That land is his garden. And then everyone will know. And you will come and see, any time, and he will know, everyone will know, that he is welcome as a stranger. But not family. You can tell them, tell your friends: I give Hengest his custom, as a stranger. And I can say to my people: look, the king is a good man, a man of his word.'

I took the point, and once we were back in London, in among all the other prettier gifts from the spoils of war, I solemnly presented the brothers with a freshly flayed ox hide. People looked askance at it.

And Hengest stretched his ox hide, all right. The Scribes heard, and told us: he cut a spiral in it with a very fine knife, and made a narrow strip of raw leather, as thin as a thread and as long as a road. And within that greasy loop he caught hills and valleys and villages, more than enough for the estate of a very great man.

'It is the custom,' was his comment. I let him have the land.

And in the midst of his new estate, Hengest reared a wooden longhouse in the Northern style, a dark and uncanny thing to call a home, with horseheads carved into the eaves and knotted dragons carved in the beams; and it stood, a stone's throw from the great earth-

works of the warlords and ancient British
kings, and the villages of the country kindreds,
and the stately country retreats where once,
on garden lawns now shabby and overgrown,
senatorial families had taken their ease, the
spoiled darlings of the long Roman peace that
was gone forever.

'You should not let British eyes see you
welcomed there as a guest. Not yet,' Maugan
advised me.

Three

The Heart of
the Storm

As a boy, I had longed to be one of the holy
people: to build my own little chapel and
hermitage in the mountains of Erith, and
live among the eagles before I died. When I grew
up and travelled east, it surprised me to learn that
such lives were not lived everywhere.

Poets, too, were becoming a common sight
again in my youth. Now I do not mean Latin

poets – Maugan told me a little about such men! I mean the real old British poets, who remembered Albion before Rome, and the old chieftains' days. Such poets had always been rumoured to be living still in the remote villages. But when I was king in London, I heard them in the streets below my windows: young men with old men's voices, and old men with young men's voices; and women, too, chanting to the crowds, and chieftains in their courts, as if Roman libraries had never been dreamt of. Chanting tightly knotted utterances, compact with wit and learning, delighting in bloodshed and the remembrance of old names: songs of Bran's head, still singing to itself as it lay buried beneath the London hills, facing across the narrow seas, and Belin, and Locrin, and all the old heroes. They stirred me to my core, and I would listen whenever I could. The church thought these songs were ungodly, but the church-priests turned a blind eye to them, for they were more tolerant then.

And now, as the troubled years passed, they were all swept up in the wind of the storm that was gathering on the coasts of Armor.

'The chief mover,' as Maugan put it to my little group of friends and advisors, 'is a bishop, a high church-priest from Gaul. Garmon, he calls himself. Bishop of,' he consulted a paper, 'Antissiodor. Over in Gaul, you see, bishops are not men of prayer, like they are here. They're chieftains. The lords of Armor like working hand-in-glove with them. And the pope of Rome indulges them nowadays too. So,' he went on, 'it would be a great prize for any Gaulish bishop to cross the narrow seas long enough to kick our British carcasses back into line. Or return Britain to the holy mother church – as they would no doubt describe it to the pope.'

'Church-priests in government,' I exclaimed. 'Madness.'

'Perhaps,' Maugan said irritably. He had heard me say such things a thousand times in the few brief years since I had crowned myself. 'But it's happening. Now –' Maugan took a breath.

'Where does that leave us? Burning at a Gaulish stake and hanging from a Gaulish gallows.' He looked round the table at my close counsellors. 'In Britain –' he went on, and hesitated. There were priests and holy men of many different orders at that table. 'Well, look at me: I've never set foot in a stone church,' he said, with a wry glance at Pelagian the Saint. Pelagian did not react. 'But I'm a priest in Britain. Just about. In Gaul I'd be a heretic. Master Bles Gwin there has been worshipping under the sky like his fathers did for generations. In Gaul, he's a heretic.'

I glanced at Gwin. He was staring into space with his arms folded, as if not hearing.

'They forgot the truth long ago in Gaul,' came the dry voice of Pelagian the Saint. Pelagian the Saint was once the best church-priest in Carleon, but I had long ago brought him to London with me, to sit at my table. 'I can tell you how the bishops of Gaul got to be princes: they told all the rich men that they could rob and murder all day from Monday to

Saturday, if they were only in church on Sunday to swallow a cleansing dose of bread. Christ himself sits mocking them from heaven. But what do they care?' He fell silent again.

'And these are the powerful friends the archbishop left London for?' I asked. 'And abducted the twin princes as he passed by?'

Maugan nodded.

'You are right, sire,' he said. 'But Amphibalus is not really the prize they're looking for. The twin princes are. Probably that's why Amphibalus took them: to curry favour,' he added.

'So why have Armor not invaded already? They have the means. And several motives, by the sound of it.'

Maugan sighed again, very heavily, and massaged his temples. He hesitated for a long time. Finally, he said: 'I don't know.' He shrugged. 'We have the Saxans now to defend us, I suppose? How much difference do Saxans really make, against the might of Armor? I really don't know, sire. I wish I did.'

I sighed, and scratched my head.

'Well. Remind me again how old the twins are.'

'About thirteen,' Maugan said.

'Nearly men, then. Do we know if they listen to these Gaulish church-people?'

Maugan could not say. 'What I will say, sire, is this: visit Hengest the Saxan in his new longhouse,' he said. 'Go discreetly, but go soon. It seems to me that you may need Saxan goodwill for some time to come. Hengest has more land-hungry kinsmen waiting at home.'

Hengest the Saxan's longhouse was like Hengest himself: a strange, vivid presence among the hills. Proud in its own dark yard it stood, with carved eaves, and the carved heads of ravens and horses at the eaves of the roof beams. We first saw it picked out in the dark by the flickering light of the torches, for Dunval my shieldman and I came to the longhouse late in the evening, before the Saxans take their main meal.

We rode up to the gatehouse. The stars of heaven above the roof suddenly seemed very strange and remote. The Saxan watchmen challenged us both, and Dunval gave them the nicknames I had chosen for us: Ganga, I called myself, while Dunval was Grim. In the tongue of the Saxans, we had called ourselves the Wayfarer and the Hooded Man. Hengest and Horsa had told me, under the stars around the campfires of the northern war, that such nicknames were used in the North, by those wishing to travel unknown.

Still cloaked, we left our weapons at the gates, as Saxan custom required, and were welcomed into the longhouse.

There were long tables within, on either side of a long, blazing hearth trench, with rows of curtained booths in the shadows behind. Many of the men were busy or idling at the tables; some I knew by sight, and they looked long and steadily at us as we approached. Around the hearth trench, there lingered still a handful of folk, Saxans and British, rich and poor.

On the throne on the dais at the far end sat Hengest. He was still dressed and armed like a seafaring robber, but he sat like a king, receiving a last few gifts and offers of friendship and service, and petitions, complaints and requests for judgment, before the evening meal was served. Welc the interpreter sat by his side. It was the way of things, I thought: Hengest was chieftain of his court with its wooden beams, just as my father had made himself lord of Carleon with its stone walls. He was making a home in Britain, and one to his own liking. People were already coming to him. The British seemed a little sullen and diffident in his presence, but it was the best I could have hoped for.

In the flickering firelight, the high rafters seemed to follow us like the crowns of trees, until we came before Hengest, and bowed in our turn, giving our Saxan nicknames. Then I looked the old villain in the face. He kept to the Saxan custom and did not acknowledge me.

'Forgive me, lord,' I said in British, 'If I cannot greet you in your own hall, in your own tongue, as I ought.'

Hengest motioned abruptly with his hand, and spoke in Saxan, and Welc asked me why

I had come. I replied that I was a weary traveller, seeking a night's rest. Then I made a point
of praising the hall.

'It is so handsome and well-made,' I told him
meaningfully, catching the Saxan idiom as close
as I could get it in British, 'a wise man would
say it was destined to stand forever.'

Hengest spoke again to Welc, who then
informed me sententiously that many a once-
proud hall was now the haunt of wolves and
ravens. Then Hengest invited us to remain as
his guests until the next morning. We shared
the evening meal at the long tables, and I felt as
if I was back at the northern wars.

We ate well at the torchlit benches, amid
the hubbub of talk, and after the meat, half a
dozen womenfolk came in from a side-chamber
to serve the drink. Strangers rarely glimpse
the women of the northern hordes. But in the
northern longhouses, even the noblest women
will wait on their menfolk at table, and the
sexes then mingle briefly almost as equals.
This is often the way in which men meet and

choose wives. In Hengest's court it was meant
as a homely touch, perhaps. The women's
faces looked weathered, but they were handsome creatures, magnificently dressed; even the
youngest, who looked about fifteen, had the
confident bearing of a much older woman. As
they moved along the tables, filling cups and
exchanging wass-hails and drinc-hails, amid the
hubbub of table-talk, they had a kind of prac-
tised ease that was genuinely graceful to watch.

I had just begun to notice that the confident young girl was glancing at me, when she
walked straight towards us, and stopped in
front of us, before the bench, and lifted the
vessel she was carrying.

She was offering to fill my cup. I raised my
cup and held it towards the vessel, as I had seen
the other men do. She filled it, glancing at me
with a kind of pride.

Then she stepped back and said something:
the familiar Saxan wass-hail. I knew enough of
their language to catch the next word; it was
cyning: chieftain, lord.

Instantly, across the hall, the table-talk abruptly ceased. There was a moment of utter silence. Your health, lord king, she had said. She had called the cloaked and nicknamed stranger a king, in the hearing of the whole court. She knew who I was: and so now, seemingly, did the whole longhouse.

The giddiness of the drink left me at once. I could not tell if it was a mistake or a challenge, or what would happen next. Dunval, sitting next to me, smelled the impending fight at once, and he bristled. Under my cloak, my hand strayed to my scabbard, and I remembered I had left my sword by the doors.

Hengest was watching, stock-still and stony faced. The girl made no movement or sign. Amid the sudden silence she was staring at me from under half-closed lids, in a kind of challenge.

Well, I thought to myself, it is for them to start the fight, if there is to be one. Pretty girl to squander a king's life for. But nobody, it seemed, was willing to draw the first sword or strike the first blow.

So I merely smiled, and lifted the cup very slowly, and drank it, and returned the greeting courteously, saying, as I had often said around the campfires: Drinc-hail. Across the whole hall, there was something like a breathing out, and the chatter started up again. The girl turned and moved away, and went with the women to wait at the tables with the same deft gracefulness as before. She had lost none of her assurance. But her eyes flickered towards me from time to time, as I watched her.

Still Hengest did not speak to us at all, or look at us.

'What was that about?' I whispered to Dunval.

Dunval glanced at me. 'Is that the old man's daughter? It looks like it. If I didn't know Saxans better, I'd say she was offering you more than a drink,' he muttered.

I shrugged. 'All women love a face with a crown above it, be it never so ugly,' I said.

When the company rose from the table, Hengest sent one of his Saxans to invite each of us to take a curtained booth for the night, apart from the mass of pallet-beds in the main hall. For appearances' sake we had to take them, once they were offered. I was on my guard.

In the night, as the hall slept in half-shadow, I lay awake, amid the snoring of Hengest's men, with the lamp lit, and Dunval in the next booth, both of us ready to fight for our lives with our bare hands. And sure enough, I heard a footstep beyond the curtain. The curtain parted, and a veiled woman slipped into the booth. She fastened the curtain behind her, and lifted her veil. Of course, it was the girl who had called me king.

I did nothing.

To my astonishment, this magnificent young woman knelt gracefully at my feet, and looked right into my eyes, with a look on her face which seemed to bespeak a kind of pride in her own desire. King as I was, no British woman had ever done as much for me in my life.

'You drank back to me,' she murmured proudly, in halting British. 'Before my father.'

Slowly, with a kind of appalled delight, I began to realise what was happening.

'You must speak to him soon,' she whispered almost casually, as if the matter was settled, as indeed it seemed that it was. 'Tell him I will be queen. He will be happy,' she added.

Then she smiled, stood, and left as suddenly as she had come, and her footsteps retreated through the snoring of the longhouse.

I lay awake all that night, thinking how strange it was that even clever women will scorn the best of men, and give their love to the worst of kings. But still I was not foolish – even though I had lived since youth with an old man's caution, through years of war and king-ship, and I remember lying awake and thinking, as if for the first time, how weary I was of it all.

It struck me nevertheless that if Hengest really did want his beautiful daughter in the British king's bed, he could not have contrived it better himself. And if he did want that, that could only mean one thing – and this, too, I could not have wanted more. It meant that he wanted to be more than a mercenary. He wanted land, and a name, in Britain.

Dunval and I left the longhouse next morning. We gave Hengest a courteous farewell; I made a point of telling him that I hoped, one day soon, to be rich and powerful enough to repay him.

'Chance-gift and late-luck let no man scorn or squander,' said Hengest, in Welc's bored, perfunctory translation.

And with that we left, but my thoughts turned back, and ever backwards on the road, towards the girl, and dwelt long on the words which only I had heard, and the gestures which had been meant for me alone.

As soon as I was back in London, I sent a herald to invite Hengest to London in person. Then I sent for Maugan, for we needed a name to put to the girl, at least. And before long the Scribes had it. The girl's name in her own Saxan tongue, as it turned out, was something like Renwein. We called her Rowena, for ease of speech, and that was what we called her when her father arrived in London to talk the matter over privately.

And that was how Rowena and I were betrothed.

To my surprise, I found that Hengest wanted the marriage to be held in secret. He wanted me to acknowledge Rowena as queen only after she had borne healthy sons. It was a strangely timid request from one who was already a hero in the North, with his own longhouse and the beginnings of lordship in Britain. But Maugan counselled caution on this point too, so I let it pass.

Hengest had one other condition.

'Put water on her head when you make her queen,' he urged me – this being what he called Christian baptism. 'Today, if you like, or tomorrow, if you like, or when you choose. And say to her now: your children will know the Christ: know him from the day that they are born. And then,' he said – finally, as I told myself, coming to the point – 'the children will be your children, and hers. They will be kings as my forefathers were: kings in Britain. But not me. I will not be king in Britain. For a man must know the Christ, to be king in Britain. And I will never know the Christ. My father's gods are heavy,' he explained, almost wistfully.

I had never heard fear in Hengest's voice before, but I heard it then, for he truly feared the devils he worshipped. And that, I supposed, was how Hengest tricked me into promising what I would gladly have given him freely: a lasting foothold in Britain, so that he would stand beside me as I went into the storm that was coming.

And I got Rowena into the bargain, a girl young enough to be my daughter; as shrewd and as foolish as I was myself, and as cold, and fragile, and unbreakable a mystery as her father. I had fathered sons and buried a wife already, but Rowena came to me unlooked for and at great cost, after life-long burdens of duty patiently borne, and she was always precious to me.

Deep in the recesses of the Molmutine Library, Maugan found a wonderful thing: a chart or map of all Albion, made of clay, in a shallow box or tray, set on legs like a large table, with the hills and rivers and towns all figured in exquisite detail, so that one saw the island as the angels of Christ themselves might see it. It was fascinating to let the eye wander over coasts and mountains and forests and fields and towns and roads, from Cernow to the wall and beyond it into the depths of the forests of Caledon. God only knew which king or lord had made this wonderful thing, and stashed it away and forgotten it in the attics of the Basilica of Concord. Such is the way of palaces, I suppose. But Maugan found it.

We set it up in the audience chamber. In little drawers around the rim, we found boxes of little men, warriors and houses and the like. We spread the little men across the toy Albion, ready to show to Hengest.

And when he came to London, Hengest was even more astonished than we had been. We spent half the night talking by lamplight in the chamber of audience, and by dawn I had begun to forge and execute my plan.

For by morning it was settled. Hengest's grandchildren would be Christians. None could really protest if the king – that is, me – settled these Christians in Britain forever, with their kindreds. On these terms, the Saxans would take the whole North and East, from the wall to Cent, with the southern shores and all their strongholds and fortresses. Some British lords would need to be cleared, but with an army of Saxans we agreed this could easily be done.

And then, at last, my own great legion of Household Saxans would have what Constantine's old troop of Household Gauls had never had: land, and a name, and a house in Albion; a place between the narrow shores for their wives and children, down all the generations to come. The Saxans would defend their portion by strength of arms, and in defending it they would protect all Britain besides, from raiding tribes and Gaulish invaders, prince-bishops and kings. The poets and free priests of Britain would stand and flourish and prosper forever behind a Saxan shield-wall. And – as it happened – my own house would also stand in the line of Rowena's children, in spite of every well-born thug and hypocrite priest in Britain. For Queen Rowena and her Christian children were to be the warrant of it all.

I never saw Maugan so excited: he had a smile on his face that nothing could move, and there was a spring in his step that amounted almost to a dance. Such things were not often seen in the black hermits, or in spies; still less in Maugan, to whom both callings were second nature. I left him doing his shuffling dance down the corridors of the Basilica, and went to discuss the marriage with Pelagian the Saint. As a gesture to my sons, I also took them into my confidence, and Vortimer had no sooner heard the news from my lips than he went alone to the chamber of audience, took a bronze lampstand, and smashed Maugan's map to fragments.

I had not expected this, even of him.

At first I appeased him. I ran after him, and bolted the door to the chamber behind us, and began to threaten and reason with him as best

I could. But it availed nothing. He was like a small child in a rage. He had thought he would be king after me: so he told me. He thought I still treasured the memory of his mother: so he told me. I was astonished. The mere possibility of such things had never occurred to me. He ran off, his weeping echoing through the palace.

I was angry, but Maugan was terrified. He bit his lip, and went as white as a sheet.

'Do you want my honest advice?' he asked, and waited. I looked at him.

'Always,' I said.

He took a deep breath, and said: 'Kill him. Kill Vortimer, quickly and quietly. He cannot be trusted to keep –'

'Are you mad?' I shouted. 'For a childish tantrum –'

Maugan held up his hands. 'I have said my piece,' he said vehemently. 'You are king. You must rule as you see fit. But I tell you this: kill him now, willingly, in time; or kill him too late, reluctantly. You must save your love now for sons that are not yet born. That's all I can say.'

And he stalked off, and wheeled on his heel as he left, and nearly spoke, but thought better of it, and left. I had never seen him so angry. I hesitated for a day, and on that day Vortimer fled from London.

For I had listened too well to Maugan, and I had looked for the heart of the storm across the narrow seas, in Gaul and Armor. But now I found that the heart of the storm was Britain's own black heart; and the rage of my eldest son was its herald. For Britain turned on me then, just as the achievement of my great purpose lay within my grasp. Before the month was out, I was fighting a war amid its ruins; not with Armor, but with my own people, the towns and villages and kindred and chieftains of Britain.

Vortimer fled to Cent. I was angry at that. And he took his brother Catigern with him, and that was more grief to me than cause of anger. The two of them were harboured by the chieftain of Cent. My other great enemy, Eldol of the dragon-hill of Carglu, soon joined them there. And then, like the traitors they were, the whole pack of them began to preach openly against my tyranny, as they called it, harping endlessly on my common birth and my friendship with pagans. I married Rowena then in haste – too much haste for a real wedding feast, even – and they called me a Saxan whoremaster into the bargain.

Warlords and chieftains danced eagerly to this rough music, and all the squabbling refugees from Constantine's Long Table flocked to the banner of the malcontents. Then all across Britain, friend stood by friend, and enemy turned on enemy, and the villagers and townsfolk, who could agree on nothing but their hatred of foreigners, gave free rein to their hatred of the white Saxans.

I desperately tried to get a message to my son Catigern through the Scribes, and sent Queen Rowena to Gwent under Dunval's safeguard, with Gwin the hedge-priest's son and Pelagian the Saint. Still the lords of Armor did nothing, and made no pronouncement, and sent no message that we heard of; why, we could not fathom. But then Garmon, the bishop of

Antissiodor, announced his intention to come to the aid of the British church, against the heretics. Bishop Garmon brought soldiers; and that settled it: there was to be a war.

I fought that war without relish, and I take no pleasure in giving an account of it.

At the outset, the Saxans and I stood alone against every power in the west: church-priests, warlords and kings, and a good portion of the common townsfolk and villagers. Hengest's brother, Horsa, came to London with all the Saxans he could muster, and other lords of the Saxans who had lately landed in Britain. We had no time to send for more help from overseas. The people of London pelted me with stones and mud before I had passed the walls; the villagers of Cent called me a false king who had sold them all to the heathens. Then they all betrayed us outright, and we were watched and stabbed and shot at and harried by night and day by unseen hands and eyes.

Meanwhile the Picts in the North and the pirates in the East shook the coasts and borders loose once more. Only the free priesthoods stood by us, and looked to us for protection; and they, of course, were quite useless on the battlefield.

Shielded by traitors among the villagers, the enemy sneaked back and forth in the silent lanes and hedgerows. For weeks we played cat-and-mouse with them. I glimpsed my son Vortimer once, sneaking through a running skirmish along the banks of the Darenth, looking pale and terrified under the thin golden circlet of his helmet; but Catigern his brother I did not see. We destroyed whole villages to smoke them out. We had no choice. But the Saxans, who were no skirmishers, grew impatient and reckless, and began to long for a pitched battle. I let them have one.

The battle was joined at the ford of Rithergabail.

The call of the gambler's luck is a call to death, but I did not begin to feel the weight and the shame of death on my shoulders, nor see the fear of death like a cloud before my eyes, until I came to the ford. Afterwards, I was never free of them.

We attacked at dawn, and the cry of *Nemethur saxa! Seize axes!* went up, muffled by the thick mist. I rode with our horsemen, and we found no quick way to cross the river, and we went out of our way, so the strength of our horses was squandered. The enemy horse then made an abortive charge, which half-broke the shield-wall, and then foundered in the mud of the river, leaving their horsemen caught up in the thick of the hand-to-hand fighting at the ford. By the time I came to the river, the levies had cut each other to pieces, and the dead lay thick for a mile and more along the banks and road. There was no victor at Rithergabail; so we lost our one poor chance, and we never got another.

At evening on the day of the battle, when the hosts had parted and withdrawn, we went to rest and drink and eat and tend our wounds, and men went out to find and count the dead. The dead were laid out in field pavilions, Briton and Saxan together, and priests were sent for. And in the night, by candlelight, we began to gather to view them: the great dead men, lolling on hurdles and trestles, still cloaked with the filth of battle.

My men never warned me. I found Hengest in the pavilion with his kinsmen and the other Saxan lords around him, and he did not greet me, for he was gazing at the dead where they lay on the trestles. Horsa, his white-haired brother, was lying there dead among them.

For a time, neither of us spoke. Then Hengest broke the silence, and there was iron in his voice.

'He waited at the shield-wall. He waited for the horses. Horsa waited for the horses! And the horses never came. But it is well, man of the west. Everyone knows. Everyone knows.'

I was listening to his words, and it was long before I looked with my eyes and saw what he meant.

And then I saw that Horsa lay beside the man who had killed him: for he and his enemy had killed each other, fighting hand to hand in the last frenzy of the battle. Some who were at the ford had witnessed the two deaths with their own eyes. The deaths were already the talk of the camp, as they became the talk of the war long afterwards. But the news was still fresh and known only to a few as I stood before the trestles, unable at first to recognise Horsa's killer by his clothing or his armour, or even his broken face. But once I saw it, there was no mistaking the rough red hair of my son Catigern; Catigern, my middle son, who had wit enough to command a horse troop before he had a beard on his cheek. And that was how I found that my son had ridden into the heart of the storm, and the storm had eaten him, and now he lay beyond its reach, in a peace which had come too late and would last forever.

For a moment as I stood before the trestles I knew nothing, and saw nothing, and heard nothing.

Even then I did not forget the crown I had taken, and I strove to keep my wits, and remain on my feet. And as I stood there, swaying, I remember clearly that I heard Hengest speak.

I paid no heed to his words. Not till long afterwards did I guess their meaning.

'It is the world,' he said. 'We should not grieve. We have new enemies now, you and I, man of the west.'

We buried them under stones, close to the ford where they had fallen, together, and raised mounds of earth above. The years have covered the earth with grass, and worn it with the wind, and the dust is scattered that once bore the names of Horsa and Catigern. In your days the stones stand broken and bare again to be seen. But they are no more broken than the ruin of greater things once seemed to me, when I was a man.

Four

The Child of Time

After Rithergabail, Hengest said frankly that the war was lost; he would not take stands any more. He fought one rearguard action after another. Our warfare ebbed towards the southern coast. Hengest added that he wanted to leave Britain, and return with more Saxans.

'I will come,' he said flatly. 'You see: I leave my blood inside you; my daughter's children that will come. I will come back for their sake.

And when I come back,' he spat, 'I will not run from any more priests.'

We marched south towards the sea.

It was a melancholy end. My beloved middle son was dead. My purpose was hanging by a thread, perhaps already broken. Inquisitors and warlord-kings were hounding us, with my devil of an eldest son at their head, helped by the villagers. Scorned and shunned, we made the coast, and shut ourselves up behind the walls of the coastal fortresses. The enemy invested the strongholds by land, but left the seas open: the quickest way to end the mockery of war which the war had become.

Even in these dark days, the indifferent sun still shone, and by its light one day we saw a sail. It was a ship of Gwent, making its way to the fortress harbour. Dunval the shield-man had come. And, to my pleasure, Rowena was with him. I was ashamed to stand before her a defeated man, but she gave no sign of reproach. She begged me to come back to Gwent, and I was glad to go, for the war was lost, and it was time to make the best of the peace, although we knew it would be a peace worse than the war.

'Hold to your luck, sir,' Dunval said. 'Things may change. Even Carglu will not come hunting for you in Carleon.'

It was not hard to muster the courage to swallow the shame, and abandon the strongholds without a fight. It was like scuttling ships: a turmoil of packing and porting and stowing and wrecking. I spoke to Hengest for the last time amid the turmoil, as we hurried along a narrow passageway.

'Your brother's blood flows in our rivers now,' I reminded him, raising my voice above the din, 'and your blood will run in the veins of our kings.'

He nodded. 'It will. The end is not yet.'

Once we had set sail, we watched the last Saxan longship turn her prow towards the far-off headlands of Cent. I did not know then if any Saxan ship would ever be seen off Britain's shores again. But if they came, I knew they would come for Rowena's sake alone. She watched until the sails sank below the horizon.

That evening, as we sailed, she smiled sadly, and said to me: 'My father says there is a worm about the world. And he bites his tail. He lives around the world, and he eats the world. And he is the world. When my father is sad, he says, the worm must eat now. We must feed him. But,' she added, looking up at me with a smile in her eyes, 'he cannot eat the whole world.'

Who knows what little bits of Saxan magic or homespun philosophy she meant; at any rate, she meant a dragon, and I had never seen any sadness in Hengest. I told her a worm in British is a little thing you would find in a garden, under the stones.

And so I sailed back to cower in Carleon, while my son Vortimer was crowned king in London.

And, sure enough, I was all but forgotten in London, I suppose; at any rate, even in Carleon, I lived quietly, and did not go openly as lord.

But peace was worse than the war as long as Vortimer was king in London, for now he was caught in his own trap. Like true Gauls, the Gaulish bishops loved a king; and like true church-priests, they loved a witch-hunt. In the king's name, bishop Garmon made martyrs of every hedge-priest and hermit he could find. He burned Britain almost clear of them. I am sure my little drummer man in London Market could never have survived.

Also, for good measure, Garmon killed many in the towns who were not hedge-priests or black hermits at all. A handful of survivors fled west, bringing tales of the horrors of the makeshift dungeons of London. But they were few. And, after a time, even that trickle ceased. And so, amid terror, and massacre, and famine, and plague and plunder, the old free priesthoods died in Albion, for the sake of a good report for a Gaulish bishop in Rome. Since my times there has been no God or Christ in Britain: at least, no Christ but the Christ of the church-priests. Somehow, Maugan survived; as, indeed, he generally did. He even passed secret messages to us through Rowena. When I asked her how they managed it, she looked at me blankly, and said: 'Maugan does it. Letters come.'

She told me that the letters came in a bag with a man who sold firewood, a short way up and down the road. How the letters crossed the Habren, she did not know. Nor did she seem to care. Maugan had arranged everything, she repeated.

'Maugan,' she informed me solemnly, 'is very dependable.'

But, she said, she was rarely present when Pelagian the Saint read the letters aloud to Gwin, and she did not know what was in them, for she could not read, or understand enough British.

So I asked Pelagian, and it was a bitter tale that he read me in Maugan's letters. Amid the turmoil, Britain's warlords and chieftains had turned on each other, and were murdered in their own wars, sometimes by the very heathens, warriors and tribesmen they had bought to settle their scores; for there were even Saxans still scattered in the remote parts of the East, among the other thieves, but they were not Hengest's people, and they had no lord but their own wills. Meanwhile, the outer tribes were making a desert of the North and East. King Vortimer was powerless, and the Gaulish bishops grew fat on the endless turmoil: it suited them to have the common people live in fear of marauders, for they would then turn all the more readily to the church for protection. So the church-priests preached that warlords and barbarians were just punishments from God, and did little to check them. And still the lords of Armor did nothing but watch. So old Albion foundered at last, the lovely child of time, at the hands of a circle of fools.

I could not sleep, for a thin, gnawing, hidden anger that smouldered endlessly, day and night. But there was nothing I could do. I could not have mustered strength enough to make war, had I taken the lordship of Gwent openly again, and summoned every friend I had in the West to my banner. All I had was my house in Carleon, and Rowena: the jewelled child of the northern longhouses and war camps, who, at the age of fifteen, had let herself go as a trophy bride to an old king, on the promise of a throne and a kingdom of her own. And, even to Rowena, I could no longer give the throne for which she hungered.

'If King Vortimer dies,' Rowena asked me lightly one night, 'will Garmon the bishop go home?'

'Garmon the bishop will go home soon in any case,' I said. 'As soon as he thinks he has beaten the British heretics.'

Then I caught her eye. It was like looking in the eye of the dragon of the world, gnawing its own tail. I knew then that my life had changed. Rowena was my destiny now, and her hunger: for I had squandered every better destiny I ever had. I said to her, deliberately: 'But if King Vortimer died, then I would take the throne again, if I could. Quickly. And then I would keep my word to your father, and give him what was rightfully his, before Vortimer and every fool in Britain went to war against me.

I would give your father a house and a name in Britain forever. And then Catigern would not have died in vain. And you, little dragon, would be queen of more than a town house in Carleon. Does that answer your question?'

She was deep in thought. 'Yes,' she said. 'It answers.'

'But for any of that to happen,' I added, sharply, 'your father must remember his old friendship with us.'

'My father gave me for his friendship! To weave the peace between you,' she said, reproachfully. I cut across her.

'Well, we had best get weaving, for there is another war at hand, I think,' I said. 'Vortimer is so weak now that it makes no odds if he lives or dies: he is a sitting target. Your father, and the lords of Armor, and the twins, and the Gaulish bishops: any of them might come, at any time, and push him off his throne. And if they do, then everything, everything I have done will be wasted.'

'Then you should go to London,' she said, suddenly decisive. 'Go to London. Sire.

And send a message to my father. Tell Maugan to send it. My father will come. He will not see me shamed. You think my father is a thief, and a coward,' she declared, 'but he is not.'

And that was enough to send me back to my purpose once again. But I was no longer driven to London by a sense of luck. I came like a returning ghost, in the emptiness of pure need.

We sent a message to Maugan, to give to his whale-hunters to send to Hengest. Then I took a small force, and crossed the angry Mor Habren, and rode to London by stealth, going from village to village and kindred to kindred, and giving a wide berth to the road.

The road in any case was overgrown and broken in places now, and there was almost no traffic on it. Many villages were abandoned, and we often had to frighten away hungry scavengers, or armed robbers. There seemed no sign of lordship or working priesthood anywhere.

We entered London by Lud's Gate, by night. The streets were deserted. The Basilica of Concord had been looted clean. The doors hung from the hinges; scraps of smashed furniture and fittings littered the broken floors. I took a torch, and left Dunval the shieldman to quarter the troops, and hurried upstairs to the library, to find it locked and barred. I was able to find a spare key, hidden in the abandoned gatehouse, and I unfastened the doors.

An oil-lamp was burning in the recesses at the rear of the library. There was a movement in the shadows, and I heard a familiar voice.

'I took the precaution of keeping the library secure,' Maugan said, sadly. 'Books are firelighters, you see. These days. But nobody seemed to remember that the library was here at all. Certainly nobody remembered that I was up here. Not very flattering. But I was safe. Welcome, sire.'

And I sat down amid the ruin of Britain, in the shadows of the library, and traded tales with Maugan the Scribe, as in the old days, as my soldiers noisily pitched camp in the echoing palace beneath us.

It was as I thought it would be: Vortimer had been poisoned; murdered by stealth. Maugan was very hesitant as he told me this. But I guessed the reason, and waved a hand. My son's last, absurd command, said Maugan, had been to order a fabulous tomb for himself among the strongholds on the southern coasts. Maugan described it as if he was trying to share a joke: a mountain of bronze, like the high places of the heathens of old. It could never have been built. Half a dozen slovenly church-priests had buried Vortimer in a tomb in the Old Temple Church. My son must have died a very lonely man.

'Don't be afraid, Maugan, old friend,' I said. 'I was a father. Not a good one, I know, but there it is: that only made me even weaker. But it is done now.' I was speaking of Vortimer, but thinking of Catigern. 'She knows I meant to bring Hengest back, if I could, so perhaps she did have a hand in it: to clear the way for her father. Perhaps others had a hand in it, too. But let me tell you a secret, old friend, in return for the many secrets you have told me.' I took a breath, and leaned in towards him, and almost whispered: 'I will never ask who killed my eldest son.' I patted his hand. 'As far as I am concerned he brought his misfortunes on himself. And on others: better men than he was.'

And then I leaned back, and waved a hand, to dismiss the matter.

'The lords of Armor are coming,' Maugan said then, quite abruptly. Then he looked at me. There was silence, for Maugan always preferred silence.

'So they have been waiting,' I said, slowly. 'Waiting until the twins were men. It couldn't be worse for us.'

And I understood; and I was afraid at last.

Maugan did not need to explain, but it was his habit.

'Now, at last, it's clear: the lords of Armor have never wanted to conquer Britain. Britain's beneath them. They want a tractable junior cousin of their own house to rule Britain for them. That's what Constantine himself was, to them. We should have seen this long ago.

'And now they have the perfect makings of two more puppet kings: the twin princes.

And it is a good time to … install them. Armor has been watching while we cleared the way for the twin princes ourselves. The British chieftains are enfeebled, and all in disarray – you included, sire, I regret to say. The Saxan lords are gone. Since the purges, the church and the bishops have the whip-hand over the priesthood in Britain – and let's not delude ourselves: they always will, now. So we have ended up doing all their work for them. The Pictish tribes are still at large. But, sire, Picts have never been much of an enemy for Armor. Remember Gralann the general. It was almost sport for the Household Gauls to hunt Picts. And now there are warships loading in the harbours along the Gaulish coasts, and men on the move, deep into Gaul. Armor will be here before long.'

I let this sink in.

'So it's simple,' I said. 'Hard, but simple. Just as it always was. We have to build a shield-wall against it. A Saxan shield-wall. And the price we pay is that the East must be a Saxan province, forever. It is necessary.'

'Let us hope Hengest lands here before the twins,' Maugan said.

Hengest came with the biggest fleet that ever sailed out of the North: a forest of dark ships, with gaping dragon-jaws and piebald sails, whipping the grey seas white. The Saxan had come, ready to seize his chance.

Rowena and I assembled the last tattered remnants of the warlords and chieftains of Britain; and the last remnants of the chieftains and warlords of the Albion of my youth – my father's Albion, and Constantine's Albion – rallied to my banner. One by one, and in twos and threes, they came, from Cernow, and the half-wasteland of Carglu, and the embattled fields of Cent. Our ragged little embassy met Hengest below the walls of Carguent.

Time had been generous to Hengest: he was king-like and magnificent now, a great man in a crimson cloak. His helm was like a crown of light, and there was gold at his girdle, and in the ornamentation of his weapons. He had no interpreter. The lords of the Saxans were with him;

some had fought beside us in Cent. The ranks of his warriors seemed to span the horizon.

'You are a king indeed now,' I said. 'I am glad to see you again. Surely I was right when I said that our dealings were not at an end.'

'And you are still a king, too,' he said. He looked steadily up and down the thin, ragged ranks of the British lords, and gave one of his shrugs, and half-turned away. His sword was half-drawn in its scabbard, but he did not handle it. It was the only time I ever saw him smile. His eyes glittered, and his face burst into wrinkles.

'When they told me your son was king,' he said, in British, to my grim pleasure, 'I came here to kill him. I do not lie. I came here to kill him, your older son.' He gave a kind of helpless gesture, brandishing his rich cloak. 'They gave me gold, and clothes. My friends and family.'

'They have killed my eldest son already,' I said.

His teeth were narrow and slanted; they were quite womanly. I noticed that he was very like Rowena in his smile. He seemed embarrassed.

'Does my daughter please you?' he asked suddenly.

'Greatly,' I said.

He sheathed his sword.

'I am here again,' he said. 'You came to me, to my house. To my hide of land. And you sat with me, and you were welcome to me. Now your sons will be kings, and they will have my blood in them. I will come to you. Let us feast the wedding,' he stammered, smiling again. 'You gave my daughter no feast at her wedding! There was too much haste. Do not shame her. Give her a feast for her wedding now. And when I have filled my belly, I will give you one more war, old friend. The greatest.'

I smiled back, and we shook hands, and ordained the wedding feast for Carcaradoc on May Day: to seal the peace between us. We parted on civil terms, and I returned to London.

Maugan at once sought a private audience. At first I thought him ill at ease, but he was excited once again, and I soon heard why he wanted to speak to me apart from the queen.

'Clearly Hengest came ready for a war of conquest against Vortimer – which would be easy for him. And he is hesitating now because he is facing a defensive war against Armor – not so easy. He is vacillating. Don't delude yourself, sire. But he may be willing to play a longer game. Is the queen pregnant? Might she be, soon? Then –' he was so excited, he could barely bring himself to say the words, 'perhaps we can see if you can wean the twin princes away from Armor. If you can ordain a marriage treaty – a settlement …' He began to gabble. 'Hengest becomes lord of the East, or most of it – the Saxan territories, but under a high king Aurel. Otherwise, more or less as planned. The queen's children cannot then be kings in London, after all. But her grandchildren might be, if we somehow married them to Aurel or Uther, or some of their children. We would have years to work out the details, if we could only get agreement in principle. But in order for the thing to work, there must be agreement in principle soon, between Hengest and the princes. As a matter of urgency. The twins are coming.

They are preparing to cross the narrow seas as we speak.' He ran a hand nervously over his tonsured scalp. 'And if that was possible, can you see the effect? Britain would have the Saxans and the Household Gauls – together, combined – an army the like of which the world has never seen, at least, not since the heyday of the legions. In a generation, a single generation, Britain could be a wasteland no longer; Britain could be a new Rome … '

'One step at a time,' I said, holding a hand up. For, suddenly, I was bored. 'One step at a time. Maugan, do me this favour: leave London. Bring every book in the library to Carleon, and lodge it there. Or as much of it as you can. Once we have had our May Day wedding feast, we will see.' I smiled. 'Perhaps one day you will teach me to read the books.'

Maugan threw himself into the preparations for May Day then, and the chieftains gathered at a monastery on the hills near Carcaradoc. The abbot was an old friend, and his refectory was an old house, a high-roofed hall of whitewashed

stone, lit by wide windows on all sides: handsome enough to give honour to host and guest
alike, but plain enough not to pique any Saxan
lord's pride in his wooden longhouse. Rowena
came, of course, and Dunval as my shieldman.
I left Gwin the hedge-priest's son in Carleon.

By May Day eve the Saxans were gathered in
tents and pavilions on the moorlands around the
monastery. They outnumbered us, of course.

The night before the feast, I cloaked my face,
and went with Maugan to Hengest's pavilion.
We talked long into the night. Hengest listened
attentively to Maugan's proposal, and nodded
his agreement. The next day, as Rowena paid
a last formal visit to her father, we made final
preparations, and assembled. Rowena came
back, looking serious, but we had no leisure to
speak, for the horns and trumpets were already
sounding, and the heralds were calling hosts
and guests alike to the wedding feast.

We left our weapons at the door of the hall,
in the Saxan fashion: heavy, beautiful, glittering
swords, a handful of red Roman steel blades jos-

tling with the jewelled eyes and golden dragon
heads of the Saxan sword hilts. Hengest was waiting for us there, and his brothers and kinsman;
and Eldol of Carglu came with me, and Gorlois
of Cernow, and Gorangon of Cent. In the clear
light from the cloister windows, warriors, Briton
and Saxan, sat in rows at the white tables, each
Briton with a Saxan beside him, sharing cups,
eating from gold on white linen. When the meat
had been served, the women came in to serve the
drink, in the Saxan fashion, and queen Rowena
came in with them, breathtakingly beautiful in
gold and white, with a cup of horn in her hand;
she came before the High Table, and spoke to me
in her own tongue, and bade me wass-hail. And
I gave her drinc-hail in her own tongue back, and
our eyes met over the cup in that hall of stone,
as they had when they met for the first time in
her father's wooden longhouse. Again, it was like
looking into the eyes of the dragon. And when
we had both drunk, she gave the cup to her father
Hengest, and Hengest rose then, and cried in a
loud voice: *Nemethur saxa! Seize axes!*

And with that the Saxans rose as one man.

I remember screaming. I remember the roar of a man in anguish, which I seemed to hear before I knew that the voice was mine, before I felt the iron grip of Hengest's arms gripping me, and his voice, louder than I remember, calling words in his own tongue. I remember a single sweeping movement of many arms, repeated down the long tables, as, in one easy motion, each of Hengest's white Saxans drew his hidden knife, and hacked down the British man next to him. I remember the clouds of British blood raining on the rich table-cloths. I remember Dunval falling. I remember the monks scattering in terror. I remember Eldol and Gorlois bellowing like boars, swinging chairs, furniture – any makeshift weapon. I do not know whether Eldol lived or died, but if he died, he died in defiance of his enemies: an old warlord, from a line accustomed to dwelling behind earthen ramparts under the sky, making havoc to the end, in a Roman house of Roman stone.

The Saxans slaughtered the lords of Albion that day, almost to a man. I was kept alive.

When the killing was over, I was brought
before Hengest, as he sat on my throne as it ran
with blood, his hands bloody on the carved chair
arms my hands remembered. Yes, I stood in the
hall, chained, a prisoner, clothed only in shame,
with the lords of Britain sprawling unmoving in
their blood in the corner of my eyes: and I saw
that as long as there were kings in the world,
it had never been any different, and it would
never be any different; and as for me, being a
prisoner was no different from being a king. So
I looked Hengest in the eye as he slouched on
my throne. His face was innocent of shame, or
any other feeling. Rowena stood next to him.
She was pale and defiant: I knew she was secretly
ashamed; perhaps none but I knew it.

'I should kill you, for my brother,' Hengest
was saying. 'But I think your soul is dead already,
old man. You ran from your own child like a
coward. I gave you my daughter to make her a
queen, a mother of kings. And you ran away, and
made my daughter a rat in a hole in the West.
And now you come to me, and say, I will make

your daughter ... grandmother of kings!' He gave a snort. 'You tell her: leave your father's gods and turn to the Christ. And Christ will make you,' he snorted again, 'grandmother of kings.'

'So I am king in London now. Hengest is king, as Hengest's fathers were kings, and Hengest will be true to his father's gods, as his fathers were true. And when the princes come from Armor, these lords, I will drive them into the narrow sea. I came to kill your son. Today I will leave your flesh to come or go as the wind blows it. Tomorrow, if I meet you, I will kill you.'

And the Saxans laughed, and when they had finished with me, they threw me out at the gate, and locked the door behind me.

And I was left alone on the moorland, and I wandered, utterly uncaring, until Maugan the Scribe came and found me.

'You escaped,' I said stupidly.

'I generally do,' he said. Then he gave a very bitter smile. 'But –'

He stopped, and looked away, and rubbed his chin, as if in thought. 'I can't go back now,' he said plaintively. 'Which makes a change. I – the books. There was no time,' he quavered. 'No time to get the books to Carleon. They're still in the Basilica. I can't –'

He tried to laugh, and waved a hand.

'It's nothing. It's over. I was a fool. Will you go to Carleon? Let's go.'

And Maugan the Scribe took me by the arm, and led me past the pavilions, out over the moorlands, under the heavy sky, past the gates of Carcaradoc; and masked and hooded, unknown and faceless, we made our way between the villages, to Carleon.

Few knew us as we passed the gates and walked the streets of Carleon. Those who knew me looked on me with wonder and fear as I made my way to the citadel.

We found Gwin, the hedge-priest's son still in the citadel, and Pelagian the Saint with him.

'We did not know if the Saxans had left you alive or dead,' Gwin muttered. He met my gaze, hesitantly. 'The twins have landed in Cent, with the lords of Armor and thousands of men,' he said. 'And Hengest must have sucked in every spare brigand and pirate there ever was in the North. All for old Albion,' he observed, with an attempt at his cocky smile. 'There's going to be a war and a half.'

Then they waited for me to speak. I sighed, and shook my head.

'Tell them to look for me in Erith. I will go into the hills, and there I will build a tower, and become a priest on the mountain if I still can, and pray for Albion a while, before the end.'

'And that will save you, do you think?' Maugan asked impatiently.

I winced.

'Save me? Who knows?' I said. 'As long as I live, I will be a threat and a reproach to them all now: the Saxans, and the twins. All of them. And they will not tolerate that. So they will come looking for me, to destroy me and mine. It is the way with such men.' I glanced at Pelagian. 'So I will go apart, far apart from the things I have loved. So if they find me, they will find me alone. That is all I can do, now.'

'Then I'm coming.'

That was Gwin. Smiling, I replied: 'Yes. Come with me. For a while at least.'

Then I turned to Pelagian. 'That means Carleon is yours now indeed, Saint Pelagian,' I said. Pelagian nodded slowly. 'So see if you can show the Gaulish bishops how a British church-priest can govern a city. For a while.' I sighed. 'Take no sides, and get a good peace for Carleon, if you can. Blacken my name to both sides if you have to; it will certainly help.'

I sighed again, and rose. 'That's all. And now let us go.'

Maugan insisted on coming with us, and I did not try to stop him. But Bles Gwin the hedge-priest's son was the guide who led us into the mountains. Gwin told me a story of his childhood then, as we walked: his father would wait indoors until the storm broke, and then run outdoors and dance in it. Gwin, as a child, had always thought it a miracle that his father never died in the rain and hail and falling fire.

Five

King on the Mountain

The three of us built a bothy high in the mountains of Erith, and dug a fire pit on the mountainside.

Far below, war came, and raged unseen. The lords of Armor landed, and met with the white Saxans to contend for the lordship of London. The fate of the island hung in the balance. Lords and kings, with banners and weapons and armies of warriors, planned, and debated, and sent out scouts and spies, and marched day and night along crumbling roads, over overgrown fields, between shrinking towns, skirmishing, fighting, looting, killing, and dying, and burning and burying the dead. Somewhere, I suppose, Rowena was still waiting on the father who, in the end, had always held her love and loyalty, for reasons that were lost now between them, in the far north of long ago.

Each day I hunted and trapped the wild beasts, gathered herbs below the treeline, and made meals ready by the fire pit before the bothy. When evening came we sat together by the fire. Fathom by fathom we dug foundations, and gathered stones, and built up course upon course of masonry. Slowly, silently, the chapel I had dreamed of as a child began to take shape: a tower where a mountain-priest could die.

I did not look for healing from the passage of time. I got none. I could not pick up a stone, to place it in the wall, without looking at the hands that held the stone, and thinking how much had been squandered between them: how much I had destroyed from what my father had left in my trust; how little truth there had proved to be within me in the end. In time, the piercing shame and horror of it became less like a living death, and more like a thin strand of life. I was thankful, until the mountain itself began to behave strangely towards us.

Maugan brought it to my attention one morning. He took me to the tower, and pointed to the walls of dry stone, a few courses high, and the heaps of loose stones lying scattered like rubble.

'There,' he said.

'What is it?' I said.

'Look,' he said. 'Look at the tower.'

'What about it?'

'The walls were higher last night. Three courses higher,' he added.

'Higher?' I said stupidly.

'Higher.'

'Why?'

'Something came in the night,' he said. 'It must have.'

'You're dreaming,' I said bluntly. I pointed. 'That was the last stone I laid, and it's there still.'

The quarrel hung in the silence between us all that day, as we worked at building or rebuilding the walls, and ate, and talked, and slept. When we woke the next day, we had the same quarrel, for Maugan was convinced the same thing had happened again in the night. It was the same the next day, and the day after that, and every day after that, until I could barely speak to him. For I could see nothing of it, and he was growing crazy with it. He began listening by night, and spoiling our sleep until we swore at him; it was as if a voice was buzzing in his ear, which made him think his voice had to be always buzzing in mine. Some dark thing was busy in the night, he said, beyond the bothy and the fire pit, undoing all the work that we were doing in the day.

Maugan then began leaving marked measuring rods by the walls of the tower at night. He would claim to have measured the height lost in the morning. As often as not, the measuring rods themselves were scattered and fallen too. This did not put him off. He simply developed ingenious systems for attaching measuring rods to the walls, and marking each stone to identify it in the morning to ascertain its movements in the night. Gwin said little, and did less; he let him get on with it.

One night I ran out of patience entirely, and set up the measuring rods myself, and fastened them to the walls, and went to bed. In the morning I had the bitter shame of admitting that Maugan was right.

It smarted more than many a greater defeat had smarted, but there was no denying it. How could I have failed to see it before? However many courses of stones we laid by day, the walls would be lower in the mornings than they were at evening, and the stones would be scattered again. It was like a dream.

After that, we watched in turns. Maugan watched first. In the morning he proclaimed, rather pompously, that he had seen visions:

silent earthquakes and terrible winds and many other suchlike portents. Now he believed that it was a devil that had taken possession of the mountain and the tower.

'The black hermits know how to deal with such things.' He glared at us with an air of challenge. I had heard nothing in the night, I might add. 'A fatherless child,' he said. 'I will leave Erith in the morning, and find a child without a father, and bring that child here, and purify this unhappy place with his blood. Only the blood will do it. The devils are satisfied with the innocent blood of their own children. Nothing else.'

We stared at him, open mouthed. But he was insistent. Maugan seemingly meant to leave the mountain, find some unfortunate bastard child, bring it back, and cut its throat over the stones. That was his prescription for settling the unsettled earth beneath the fledgling walls.

'I know it sounds harsh,' he added, with a glimmer of his old urbanity.

I glanced at Gwin.

'Let him go in search of his innocent blood,' Gwin said heavily. 'I know just where he might find a fatherless child. Don't worry, sire. I'll go with him. There will be no trouble, I promise you. I've heard such things before.' He waved a hand vaguely. 'Devil's children. The black hermits have always believed in them: children of women and the demons of the middle air, or some such. I never knew they were so useful in settling earthquakes,' he added dryly, 'but you live and learn, I suppose.'

'It is Christ's work,' Maugan insisted. I was shocked and angry.

'It is sarabaite's work,' I rejoined. 'I will not forbid you to leave, Maugan, since you did not come here at my command. But I command you now: there is to be no bloodshed. Do you understand? You are to harm no children. Fatherless or otherwise. Do you hear?'

'Yes, king,' he sneered, for all the world like an old torturer deprived of an expected victim. It was not like Maugan. He had always been piti- less at need, but I had never known him be petty.

Maugan left the next morning, and Gwin went with him. I watched them go anxiously, and remained behind, to build and rebuild.

Still I would wake in the mornings to find the walls broken and scattered. I all but abandoned the work.

In time, Gwin and Maugan came back with a woman, and a child, a boy. He looked about ten. The woman was a nun, pale and pinched but still comely enough, with crow's feet around her dark sloe-eyes: some nobleman's daughter, sent to the cloister for her family's convenience. She was sullen and suspicious. I supposed Maugan had put some spell on her, or pretended to, since people feared the curse of a black hermit. The boy was a gangling red-haired monastery brat, at once feral and precocious: an infant Constans. He came clinging to his mother's habit. Maugan brought them to meet me at the foot of the tower. Alongside the two of them, he suddenly looked every inch the old mountain-priest.

'A fatherless boy,' said Maugan with grim satisfaction. 'Here. We found him.'

I looked at the mother.

'Are you are the king on the mountain?' she asked. I glanced at Gwin, who gave me a quick nod.

I snorted.

'I suppose, if that is what they call me now, yes,' I said.

'Why are we here? What are you going to do with us? I will curse you with God's curse if you or your men harm my child,' she said, defiantly.

I sighed, and took them to the bothy, and fed them from the fire pit. They ate ravenously, for Maugan had been driving them hungry.

Then I learned the story. Maugan had gone to Carleon, which was weathering the war pretty well. He had spoken with Pelagian the Saint and then gone searching with Gwin's help. They had gone west, to Mordun, a town of fishermen, and found the boy in the streets, amid a huddle of jeering boys. The boy had been the butt of the whole town ever since his birth, which had set every tongue wagging, and Maugan soon found a way to his mother, who was living in a cell a little way apart from her sister-nuns. Neither mother nor son wanted anything to do with Maugan, until he tried telling them that he served the king on the mountain. And this title, dreamed up by Maugan quite on the spur of the moment, had pleased the boy very greatly; and for that reason alone, the two of them had come back with him.

I hesitated, and sighed, and addressed the mother.

'He has brought you here,' I explained, pointing to Maugan, 'because he thinks your child has no father.'

She looked away, tight-lipped, and, to my astonishment, she nodded.

'How can that be?' I asked, with a glance at Maugan, who was eyeing the child intently.

'Ask them in Mordun,' the woman said, with contempt. 'Everyone thinks they know who it was. Because every one of their husbands would love to get in among the nuns, if they could.' She raised her head, and went on: 'I was not always

a bride of Christ, king on the mountain. I was
born a king's daughter, and I know what a man's
love is. His father,' she indicated the child, 'was
no man. He was a devil from hell. Such things
come and go in the convent as they please.'

I was still wondering silently at that, when
Maugan said, venomously: 'I told you so.'

The boy began crying. There is something
terrible about the weeping of boys. The woman
started when she heard it, and drew her child
to her. I saw at once that she was terrified and
dangerous, truly ready to kill for him. I spoke,
quickly and forcefully.

'I am king on this mountain, and I have for-
bidden bloodshed here. They know it, and you
know it. You are safe.'

'You knew!' the mother hissed. 'Your men
wanted to kill us. And you knew.'

With one angry movement, she swept the
child up and fled. I scrambled out after her.

She was yards away, making for the path-
way down the mountain. Then, with a sudden,
wordless scream, the boy tore himself away

from her, and started stamping his feet crazily and bellowing a single word, chanting it over like a drumbeat: 'Vortigern! Vortigern!'

He was screaming my name to the sky. The woman was staring at him.

I stared at the two of them.

'Vortigern!' the boy screamed again.

'Stop!' she shouted.

And the boy stopped.

There was a silence. He stood still, looking up at his mother with a beseeching gaze, sobbing and writhing where he stood, like a much younger child struggling to hold its water.

Then the woman turned to me: 'Are you Vortigern?'

I nodded.

'If you touch him, you or your black hermits, I'll kill you,' she said.

'I know.'

'Then,' she said, 'we were right to come.'

And before long we were all back in the bothy, and she was holding the boy's unmoving head in her lap, coaxing him to speak.

'Vortigern is here,' she explained gently. 'Look. There he is. That's him. That man over there. You can speak to him now.'

There was no response.

'Tell me, then. Tell me. I can tell him. Tell me and you'll feel better, I promise, say it and you'll feel better. You always do, don't you – remember? Tell me.'

Still with his head in her lap, he muttered: 'There are devils here. And worms, and dragons. I hate them.'

She glanced at me then.

'They are devils and worms everywhere,' I said, to my own surprise. 'Always.' And there comes a time when there is no more strength to bring to bear against them. And then the dragon takes the mask from its face.

I believed I had said this aloud, but it was only a thought.

The boy lifted his head, and half-turned his face towards me.

'King Vortigern. Your walls fall down,' he said. 'That's why that man wants to kill me.

He thinks blood will stick the stones together. It's stupid. Stones are too heavy.'

'I know,' I said, with a wry smile at Maugan, who was listening, stony faced. 'I told him so myself. I did,' I added, with a glance at the mother. 'But he would not listen.'

The boy made a sudden movement: he was curling up on the bedding. 'Under the walls,' he murmured. 'The dragons are sleeping in the water under the walls. They wake up at night and fight.' He had his thumb in his mouth like an infant, and I realised he was speaking to his mother. 'It's all right, King Vortigern won't kill us,' he told her drowsily.

Before long, he was fast asleep.

'When he says something like that, King,' she murmured, 'it's always true. He had it from his father,' she added. 'Devils never lie.'

I left her to rest in the bothy with her child. I set Gwin to watch over them, at a discreet distance. Then I told Maugan: 'We need to dig the foundations again. Around the tower. We will do nothing else, till that is done. Scour it out. Something's the matter with the foundations.'

We spent the rest of the day digging. At evening the water collected in a dirty, ragged-edged pool between the stones. We found nothing else, and we dug until we were exhausted. I could tell Maugan was thinking that I was taking my revenge for the measuring rods.

That night, I told Gwin and Maugan to sleep by the fire, and leave the bothy to the woman and her son. It was a mild night, but I could not sleep for thinking about the woman's words, and I sat wide awake above the half-built ruins, where the dew and rainwater collected in a pool in the freshly dug earth, and I watched the black shadow of the mountain's head rearing above me, and the stars wheeling in their stations beyond it.

Maugan had always lacked sentiment about the shedding of blood. We all had; I had fought wars, and done worse things than kill one defenceless mother and child.

For such things are easily done, when it comes down to it; truly, they are too easily done.

Fool and failed king as I was, I listened then attentively to every small noise of the mountainous earth around me, the hall of dark and silent stone whose roof is the world on which we walk, wondering what she thought of us who scurry about her, in search of the peace she keeps to herself.

And, listening, I heard it.

I cannot easily say what I heard; it was so like silence. But there were tiny waves lapping at the lip of the pool; no greater than if a small fish had leapt for a fly above the water. The lapping grew insistent. Stray droplets began to sprinkle my feet. The night breeze began to quicken. I could not help but stare at the dark water which I could barely see.

And by some trick of the dark my staring eyes began to see vague, formless things moving in the darkness above the restless pool, shouldering the dark air aside to hover on the troubled face of the water.

I cannot easily say what forms I saw there. They seemed to be the size of a man and more than the size of a man, and to my dazzled eyes they gleamed with a depthless half-light, like clouds of twilight.

There were two of them: one dark with a red, ember-like sheen; and its twin ghostly pale, like mist. I watched in wonder.

Suddenly I felt giddy, and I thought the earth was spinning. The light within the twin forms was kindled to sharp, flickering flames of red heat and white heat. The forms were convulsed, and writhed and reared themselves upright together, matching the dark summits of the hills in size, and then outmatching them, to eclipse the stars, as each lifted its own gaunt, cavernous head to grieve and exult above the mountains, and scatter the stones of the earth below.

And that was how I saw with my waking eyes the thing I had dreamed, and sought, all my life, in love and fear, and held numbly in my hands for a little while, as the masks fell from the faces of the dragons.

The great dragons danced for no longer than the blink of an eye, as it seemed. For the world is only a tissue of masks and veils; and when the veils are lifted, in birth or death or the other ecstasies, we look beyond them, and see faces that we already know, but cannot bear to look at for long. For no more than an instant then, all veils were lifted before my eyes, and face to face, I glimpsed the adorable and pitiless mystery at the heart of war, and love, and desire, and grief, and the passing glory and squalor of our lives, and the endless wonder of the created world.

But they were at war, and the war of the dragons was eternal; it had lasted since the beginning, and it would last until the end.

And then I heard voices: voices which were sharp with grief, and angry, and exultant; and I knew at once that they were the voices that had hummed in Maugan's ears in his private torment, waking and sleeping, days and nights past.

'Give us the child,' the voices said. 'The fatherless child. Give us its blood. Give us its white hide. Look at us! Are we not more to you than a fatherless child? We will serve you if you give it. The stones will serve you, if you give it. The world will serve you if you give it, and the mystery of the world will serve you, and you will be no mere father, but a true king at last. We never lie. Give us the child.'

The anger and grief and exultation in the voices was almost unbearable, for each twin dragon would court its own death, and seek the death of its twin, and so live and die, and know birth and rebirth, time and again, forever, and this was the war which had shaken the tower walls which had buried them as they rose and fell, and were built and rebuilt. I broke into a sweat and cried out, and heard a desolate sound, very close at hand.

It was the boy crying once more.

I turned, and looked back.

The boy was crying in the dark, a little way off.

I gasped, and shook myself.

I was still sitting by the ruins, and it was bitterly cold. The wind had gone through my thin cloak, and my limbs were numb. Now the sky foreshadowed the dawn, and the east shone pale, and the walls of the tower lay scattered in the half-light, and there were no dragons; the mystery had drawn its veil down over its face again. I felt empty and ashamed and relieved, and bereft.

'Give you the child?' I heard myself muttering aloud, into the vast silence that cloaked the empty mountain. 'King at last? That would have been a tempting offer. Once. Christ, the folly. The sheer stupidity of it all.'

I sighed, and rubbed my legs, and stretched. That one glimpse had lasted the whole night.

The boy was stumbling noisily up the hill towards me now, through the chilly morning twilight. He seemed to be in a world of his own. He came to the place where I sat. I was about to speak to him, to ask him if he had seen any dragons. But he walked past me without seeing me, as if he was walking asleep.

Then, to my alarm, he stumbled and fell, a little way off. I heaved myself to my feet and hobbled after him. When I caught him up he was writhing on the ground a little, muttering in a low undertone. I leaned over and caught the words. There was something about the white dragon and the red dragon, and then something like: 'The high chief will burn between nectar and fear. The chief of the great worms will kill the white mane. The bear of the wood will drive the white herd …'

And so forth. I thought best to let him talk himself out, so I threw my cloak over him and listened a good long while to his mutterings. It was like poetry at first, good to listen to; but very dark and unclear. I paid little enough heed to it at the time, but afterwards I found I remembered it, or much of it.

At any rate, the boy soon fell silent and lay still. His eyes were half-open and the breeze played in his hair.

'Not hard to read were those riddles of yours, boy,' I said, loudly, more to myself than to him. 'I know my own people: the Britons. We are like the red dragon. The white dragon is the Saxans. Is that not it?'

He blinked. I saw at once that his eyes were flickering towards me.

'So, boy,' I asked. 'Are you with us? Can you tell me who is the high chief? Or the bear of the wood? Is it Uther? Or Aurel, maybe? One of the twins?'

Then he whispered hoarsely, his gaze still steady: 'Uther's son.'

He settled his head more comfortably on the cold stones. Still he did not look up. He murmured, more clearly: 'Uther's son will be a great king. He will drive the Saxans into the sea.'

I have to say, I winced a little at this.

'And will you help him do it, then?' I asked, with the best grace I could muster.

The boy said gravely: 'I am his priest.' Then he closed his eyes, and seemed to go back into his trance a moment; then he opened his eyes again. 'There,' he said. 'Like that. That is me. I am sarabaite, black hermit to the great king. I will be his soul. My father gave me no name, for my father does not give names. They will have to call me: the one who came from

Mordun. But they will speak of me in Armor before the end, and then everyone will call me Merlin. Silly Merlin. It is a silly name. I will be lonely forever, but there is no help for it.'

'Merlin?' I said, diffidently. 'It sounds like a story. Like a dream. A pretty foolish dream at that.'

'It will be,' the boy said, 'when I am dead.' He gave a shallow sigh. 'But it isn't now.'

I hesitated, and looked down at him.

'You will be dead sooner than you think, if you lie there on the cold ground,' I said.

He sighed again, and lay still, his eyes still open.

'I had sons,' I found myself explaining. 'You always want to help them. Always. No matter what happens. Even if you cannot help them. Even if you don't know it yourself. Even if they're just fools. And I could not help mine. I could not. And they are dead.'

I felt a catch in my own throat as I spoke.

I breathed deeply, and strode around stamping my feet for warmth. I felt light-headed after my strange night, and it was odd too to be lectured on my own failure with such authority by such a child.

But like many forthright children he seemed to mean no ill by his honesty. I went to wake his mother, and the five of us took a morning meal: the only meal we would all eat together.

And so, by the grace of the child's words, and the gift of his foresight, I already knew that it was time to prepare for the end of the war, and the end of many other things besides.

And that morning I released the woman and her child, and offered them an escort to Carleon. As they made ready to leave, I spoke with Gwin and Maugan for the last time, and told them everything, and they understood.

With Maugan I sent my best memory of the boy's sayings in the night, and the command to commit them to writing as soon as he could. He was most intrigued, and promised that he would do it; he seemed to think the boy might help him with it. I said nothing, but I did not think the boy would want to do that, even supposing he could remember what he had said himself, which I did doubt. But I left them to arrange things. I think the boy's sayings were written down eventually, and some learned men thought them great prophecies. But I never heard the outcome of it. As I say, I have never understood books.

With Bles Gwin, the hedge-priest's son, I sent nothing but my love. He was too much of a coward, in the best sense, to face what we both knew was coming for my tower and for me. He loved life still.

'You must live,' I told him. 'Silly Merlin will need a teacher.'

The woman was always a little unsure of us. But the boy threw his arms around me, and buried his face in my own robe, as he had his mother's, and wept inconsolably.

'Come with us,' he pleaded. 'I love you.'

'Then I love you too, child,' I told him, without thinking. And having said it, I knew that somehow, quickly and mysteriously, it had become true. 'But I have to stay here. You see, there are men looking for me. They will come here in the end. I cannot leave; they would only follow me. Don't you see? Ask your mother,' I said, with a glance at the nun.

She nodded slowly. 'Come on,' she insisted, holding out a hand for him to take.

'Are they going to kill you?' the boy asked.

'They'll try. So who knows. We'll see. If I can, I'll follow you down and catch up with you.' You won't, I thought to myself, even as I spoke.

He shook his head, and hugged me as if he meant to cut me in two with his arms.

I cajoled him as best I could, telling him we would be free priests together, like brothers, needing no speech or sight of one another, so there was no need to mourn.

And I told him that Bles Gwin, who was going down with him, was a far better hedge-priest than I. But he was already growing calmer.

When he went to take his mother's out-stretched hand, I told them I would walk out awhile in the hills, to gather stones. When I came back to the bothy, all four of them were gone, and I saw them no more.

I did weep that day, for the last time.

Afterwards, I set to work again in silence, turning over the memory of the boy's dark sayings as the days passed. And I raised new courses of stones under the turning sun and the running clouds, and the unblinking blue sky of day, and the wheeling stars of night. I saw no dragons, and I laughed at the thought of them, for each day's work now lasted beyond the following dawn. Day by day the walls rose. I built a new tower, a handsome thing, and I roofed it over, and it stood against wind and weather.

And far below the war raged on, as kings and priests shed fruitless blood as mortar for their crumbling walls; while all the time beneath their feet, unseen dragons slept and woke and slept, with their terrible faces veiled under the silent earth. I understood that Hengest would die, and Aurel would die, and Uther would die at last, long years after he had ransacked the mountain to find me, so that I could die in my turn. The monks and chroniclers would record that I betrayed Constantine; Constans; Albion;

Rome; the church of Christ; I betrayed Horsa;
I murdered my son Vortimer; I courted Albion's
enemies, and God's, and became their play-
thing, and ran and hid in the mountains until
they hunted me down. But only a fool would
dream that one can betray as I betrayed, and
spilled blood as I spilled it, and go scot-free.

But then, at last, the greatest of the kings of
old Albion would come. And by his side would
stand a priest without a name, one who came
from Mordun: the last and the greatest churchless priest that Albion would ever know.

And together they would hold the white
Saxans at bay, and put aside the Long Tables of
their fathers, and set up a table that was round,
without a head or a foot; a meeting place for
fellowship without rank; and they would deal
fairly and keep faith, and so kindle a light in
Albion that the worst bishop or Saxan could
never quench, and a glory that will beguile the
world until its ending.

But I have ceased to thirst for consolation.
I have entered my tower, and barred the door,

and climbed the stair to the upper room, and sat at the window to listen in stillness to the mountain lark, and pray to the great God for the salvation of Albion, and await the coming of the fire.

It is long years now since I heard the voices of the twin princes' men below the high window. The pain of the burning was bitter, but it was brief; and the tower is fallen, and the fire is long cold. Rain and wind have cleansed the ruin of the smoke and ashes, and my ashes were mingled in among the smouldering rubble, and they, too, have been cooled and washed away by the wind and rain. Rome herself is a memory, and her fall is all but forgotten, and the agony of the dark years that were my years, the years of my life and my death.

Only the silence has lasted.

And that you can still find, in your days, if you know where to search among the western mountains, amid ruins which seem of no account, where it seems that the echo of some strange voice is just falling silent.

If you enjoyed this book, you may also be interested in…

Denbighshire Folk Tales

FIONA COLLINS

Fiona Collins has collected a wide range of tales here. People unfamiliar with the culture and customs of the county will find some fascinating and unusual tales. Denbighshire has inspired stories of magic, dragons and devils and ordinary people doing extraordinary things.

978 0 7524 5187 9

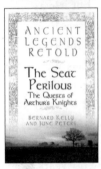

Ancient Legends Retold: The Seat Perilous

JUNE PETERS AND BERNARD KELLY

The Seat Perilous was the place left for the knight who would one day attain the Grail. These are the untold tales of the knights who went out into the world and the ladies of the lake they found there.

978 0 7524 8970 4

Ancient Legends Retold: The Legend of Pryderi

FIONA COLLINS

Pryderi is a figure from the earliest days of Welsh legend. The stories tell of a great warrior; a hero of the battlefield, who inhabited a world of magic and might. In this book, his legend is retold for a new generation.

978 0 7524 9005 2